"Craig's creativity on the grill and knowledge of fire use is remarkable. This book delivers his tasty recipes to your home. With easy-to-follow instructions and a great variety of dishes, you are going to want to grill every night!"

—**LINKIE MARAIS**, yacht chef, *Food Network Star* (Season 8)

"Craig's passion for grilling anything and everything shines through amongst these pages. Sit back, give it a read and grab a napkin to keep the drool off the pages!"

—**CHAD ROMZEK**, creator of Kick Ash Basket®

"This book is a must-have for anyone who wants to broaden their cooking knowledge, create unbelievable recipes and 'WOW' their guests!"

—**CHRIS GENTRY**, Gentry's BBQ & General Store

"This book is a must-own for anyone who wants to elevate their live-fire cooking game!"

—**SHANE DRAPER**, pitmaster of Draper's BBQ

"This book is a spectacular collection of well-written recipes, specific methods and stunning photography."

—**BOB HACK**, Sales and Marketing Manager, Flame Boss®

"For any Big Green Egg enthusiast (or any Kamado lover!), I highly recommend picking this book up and learning from Craig how to level up your Kamado game!"

—**STEVE McELROY**, creator of Stoked on Smoke

"Craig's well-written methods and recipes—written in layman's terms—will not only enable you to create tantalizing dishes, but will lead you into a deeper understanding of Kamado-style grills."

—**JEFFREY B. ROGERS**, creator of The Culinary Fanatic

MASTERING THE
BIG GREEN EGG®
BY *Big Green Craig*

AN OPERATOR'S MANUAL AND COOKBOOK

PAGE STREET
PUBLISHING CO.

PAGE STREET
PUBLISHING CO.

First published in 2020 by

Page Street Publishing Co.

27 Congress Street, Suite 105

Salem, MA 01970

www.pagestreetpublishing.com

The "Big Green Egg" is a registered trademark of Big Green Egg, Inc.

Distributed by Macmillan, sales in Canada by The Canadian Manda Group.

24   23   22   21   20   1   2   3   4   5

ISBN-13: 978-1-64567-024-7

ISBN-10: 1-64567-024-4

Library of Congress Control Number: 2019943011

Cover and book design by Ashley Tenn for Page Street Publishing Co.

Photography by Ken Goodman

Printed and bound in the United States

Page Street Publishing protects our planet by donating to nonprofits like The Trustees, which focuses on local land conservation.

Dedication

This book was written in memory of my little brother, Derek. You are my inspiration for food perfection. I hope you are watching from above and like what you see. I miss you.

CONTENTS

INTRODUCTION

I have grilled and smoked for most of my life and have always enjoyed the craft. A gas grill is convenient to use for a quick midweek meal. In August 2009, I hauled a $500-ish "stainless-steel" gas grill to the curb for the trash collectors to pick up because it had rotted through and was falling apart. This was gas grill number three over the course of about six years that had died and gone to live in the landfill. I felt that there had to be a way to stop the bleeding of money that I was throwing away *and* an easier way to generate a high-quality barbecue product. A few days later, I was explaining my frustrations to a friend of mine, and that's when he opened my eyes. "I've got this ceramic grill thingy that I fire up on a Saturday night, put on some meat, wake up the next day and, abracadabra, barbecue!" I explained that there is no way that this could be possible. I had to see it with my own eyes. Enter Kamado-style cooking.

I started researching these "ceramic thingies" online and found a killer deal on a used Big Green Egg on Craigslist. The ad was for an XL Egg that was heavily seasoned, which is exactly what I was hunting for. I went to meet the guy selling the XL Egg, and it ended up following me home that day. Superexcited, I immediately visited my local big-box store to pick up supplies to build a table. Commence table construction! After an exhausting weekend, I was finally ready to fire up this "ceramic thingy." I was blown away with how little attention this cooker required during low and slow barbecuing. Ribs and pork shoulders were a breeze and a family favorite. However, that was the extent of what I was cooking at the time.

In March 2010, my wife walks in and says, "That's it, I'm done. I'm never cooking again. I hate it. It's just way too much work and I've lost my passion for it. From here on out, it's frozen dinners for us." This conversation was much longer than that, I promise, but I gave you the Craig's Notes version to save you the boring details. This was a *real* problem in the Tabor household! I don't think y'all understand! My wife's family is Italian. Her grandparents emigrated from Naples, Italy, in the 1920s and settled in one of the Italian burbs of Chicago. There was never a shortage of food around her family. I just couldn't see how this was going to work with Stouffer's frozen dinners! HAHA! I was at a fork in the road: Do I turn in the direction that leads me to frozen food *or* do I turn the other way and assume the role as the family cook?

Obviously, you know which turn I took because you are still reading this book. I did assume the role of the family cook, but could my family live on ribs and pulled pork? The answer is yes, but that would get really boring after a couple of weeks. At that point, I was not using the cooker deemed "the ultimate cooking experience" to its fullest potential. It was time to step up my cooking game.

From this point forward, I started broadening my horizons and challenged myself to cook something new every time I lit a fire. I added all sorts of new proteins and started using different cooking methods and techniques. Every day was full of research and recipe planning. I was on my path to learning how to make a Kamado cooker sing. Like everyone, I experienced fires going out, smoky-tasting pizza, grease fires, dirty smoke, burnt gaskets, frustration with temperature control, spiked temperatures, running out of charcoal, cracked pieces of ceramic and everything else that comes along with cooking on a Kamado cooker and slowly learned how to combat these issues.

I started posting pictures of what I was cooking on Facebook long before it was the cool thing to do. My wife urged me to take those posts to another social media platform. I opened up a Twitter account and started posting there under the name @bgewithcraig. Instagram was next. As my cooking and photography skills increased, so did my following. People started noticing that I possessed a high level of quality and enjoyed the content. A good friend of mine decided that I needed a branded logo and designed one using a play on words, and so the Big Green Craig brand was born. As the Big Green Craig project began to gain steam, I started to become friends with some really cool people who shared my interests and passions in the grilling, smoking and barbecue world.

I started attending grilling and smoking festivals known as Eggfests. An Eggfest draws groups of enthusiasts who share their food and recipes. The festival is traditionally put on by a hardware store, a butcher shop or a grill shop that sells Eggs. These events are very cool for someone on the fence about getting into Kamado cooking. Big Green Egg calls its main event Eggtoberfest, and it is held in the fall every year in the Atlanta metro area. This is a megaevent with tons of teams, tons of attendees and lots of fun. I packed up the family and dragged them down to the 2013 Eggtoberfest event. The festival was fine, but I was sort of disappointed in several things. The quality level of food served was middle of the road. There were very long lines as well. Several times, I would be the next person in line for a sample, only to be told that they had run out of food. While I understood why these things were happening, I couldn't help but think how I would do things differently.

In 2014, I captained a team and we cooked at the Eggtoberfest event. The team was assembled from some of the great people I had grown to be friends with through social media. Knowing we were going to cook all day in a parking lot, I knew that I needed to recruit cooks that had the knowledge and possessed the talent to fly in and do just that. Some of the original team members came in from Missouri, Tennessee, Texas and Georgia and even included two Pitmasters featured on the TV show *BBQ Pitmasters*. We did decide to enter the People's Choice contest with a one-off recipe I wrote called the Just da Tip Roll. This was a tri tip sushi roll that blew people away. What, you've never had grilled sushi? Ha! We came into this event with enough sushi roll components to feed all 5,000 people in attendance so that everyone there got to taste our tip. We came in second place.

In 2015, the team grew and so did the production. We cooked what I call a Piglet Popper. A Piglet Popper is a smoked pork belly burnt end, corn dog battered, deep-fried, served with a super sweet barbecue sauce and a pickle chip. We served up over 160 pounds of pork belly, if I remember correctly. It was awesome watching people wait in our line three or four times for the same bite. We won first place that year. We won first place again in 2016 with a monster team! We served up a recipe I call Jailhouse Rocks. As a tribute to Elvis Presley's favorite sandwich, this was grilled banana cookie dough that was deep-fried, covered with smoked candied bacon and then drizzled with a peanut butter glaze. At one point, our line was over an hour long with people waiting for these tasty treats. Rumor has it that Ed Fisher himself, creator of Big Green Egg, even loved the Jailhouse Rocks!

Both of these first-place wins really started opening a lot of doors for me. I started to get invites to come demo at Eggfest and events all over the world. Companies started to hire me to write recipes for them and to run some social media campaigns. I've cooked next to Chris Groves (www.nibblemethis.com), judged with Big Moe Cason, dined at legendary chef Ted Reader's house and even sailed on a Royal Caribbean cooking cruise! (I won their grill-off, by the way.) Needless to say, all the social media exposure, the two Eggtoberfest wins and appearing at dozens of Eggfests all over the world made me *the* Big Green Egg authority. In 2018, I achieved Delta Medallion status from all the barbecue events I had been invited to that year, with events in Canada, in Hawaii and all over the continental United States.

Now you know how I fell into cooking, how it's become a full-time side job and what gives me the validity to be a Big Green Egg authority and be able to share with you what I've learned over the years, as well as some killer recipes. There is a saying where I come from, "There's more than one way to skin a cat," which rings true in all of grilling, smoking and barbecue. The methods, the tips, the tricks and the thoughts behind them that I am sharing may not be the only way, but they have yielded terrific results for me.

Craig Tabor

FIRE, FIRE!

So, what's a Kamado? Many people argue and credit Big Green Egg for being the first Kamado ever invented. Well, they are wrong. Kamado cooking dates all the way back over 3,000 years ago, to the ancient Japanese. *Kamado* is the Japanese word for "stove" and literally means "place of the cauldron." The Kamado was meant to be more of a movable cooking vessel rather than a stationary cooker in a kitchen. U.S. soldiers were exposed to Kamado-style cooking during World War II. Ed Fisher, founder of Big Green Egg, was one of the first in the United States to experience the difference in Kamado cooking and decided to create his own venture now known as the Big Green Egg.

KAMADO COMPONENTS AND ACCESSORIES

Today's modern Kamado-style cookers vary slightly in fit, finish, accessories, luxuries and profiles. However, they all seem to use the same basic ceramic components. They each have a vented base unit, hinged dome with temperature damper, fire bowl or box and cooking grate. A ceramic diffuser is optional to create a true indirect cooking chamber. The simple theory is to create a fire in the bottom of the cooker while the rounded dome lid creates convection. The amount of oxygen allowed through the bottom vent and the volume of carbon dioxide by-product escaping from the top damper controls the internal cooking temperature. I'll discuss this more in "Fire: How Everything Works" (page 16). I'll be using four different Kamado cookers in this book: a Big Green Egg, a Kamado Joe, a Grilla Grills Kong and a Slow 'N Sear Kamado.

The modern Kamado cooker has become more than a necessity, and some have even turned it into a hobby. The thought of someone ten years ago having multiple of these pricey cookers was unheard of, but is extremely common by today's standards. (I think I had six at one point. Ha!) And the businesses that thrive within hobbies are the accessory companies. As with any hobby, everyone wants to enhance performance, personalization and fun toys. Premium charcoal, performance-boosting charcoal baskets, custom tables, fire-controlling computers, fire starters, thermometers and cast-iron cookware are accessories that every modern Kamado enthusiast wants.

Here are some of the aftermarket accessories that I really believe make the cooking experience better:

- **FOGO Lump Charcoal:** A Kamado needs to be fueled by natural lump charcoal. This charcoal burns clean and hot and provides a neutral flavor that allows me to control the flavor of smoke that I want on my food.

- **Kick Ash Basket:** The KAB is an ash tool, not a charcoal tool. This basket aids in cleaning out the ash from the cooker, but most important, improves airflow into the fire chamber, helping the fire breathe.

- **JJGeorge cedar tables:** Although a metal stand will work, a gorgeous cedar table looks fantastic, provides you with much more room for prep work and staging and gives the cooker a refined look.

- **Flame Boss:** This electronic fire computer maintains your fire during long cooks. Although I highly recommend learning to use your Kamado without one, a Flame Boss is definitely an advantage to a seasoned cook.

- **Fire starters:** Some people use paper and oil, but I am a huge gadget guy, so I prefer a Looftlighter, a JJGeorge Grill Torch or a FOGO Tumbleweed to get my fire started. Any of these are way quicker than rubbing two sticks together.

- **Thermometers:** This is probably one of the most important accessories a cook requires. A proper thermometer is what keeps your food finishing at the exact right temperature and will enhance your dining experience. ThermoWorks makes the industry-leading thermometers; I suggest purchasing both a wired thermometer and an instant-read. Spend some money on these and you'll be very happy that you did.

- **Cast-iron cookware:** This sounds old school, like your grandparents' cookware. However, cast-iron cookware broadens your abilities on the grill, stands up to the high temperatures of the grill and adds one more tool to your toolbox. Lodge Cast Iron makes some very cost-friendly cookware.

FIRE: HOW EVERYTHING WORKS

Add flame to charcoal and *fire,* right? Well, sort of. Here is what is actually happening. Fire is a chemical reaction that needs three things: heat, fuel and oxygen. Heat will start the fire, the fuel is what burns and the oxygen makes it breathe. Oxygen creates oxidation and causes the fuel to burn. Rapid oxidation to combustible fuel makes fire. Fire's main goal is to consume fuel as fast as it can. Let's make it even simpler and discuss building a campfire. You create some heat with a spark, kindling (fuel) combusts and the oxygen allows the flame to grow. Adding more fuel increases the size of the fire, generating more heat.

Let's think about that for a second. A bigger fire generates more heat? Hmmm . . . maybe we should be building fires in our Kamados based on the heat that we want to use to cook? (Okay, maybe I set that up a tad. . . .) Many people cooking on Kamados light their fire the same way regardless of what temperature they want to use to cook. I teach all of my students in my grilling classes to build their fire based on the temperature that's required for their recipe. If I want to smoke low and slow, I build a small fire; and if I want to sear at high temps, I build a big fire. Building a 600°F (315°C) fire when you want to smoke at 225°F (110°C) is going to cause you a lot of problems. Building such a large fire will consume so much fuel that you will run out of it and really grow to dislike Kamado cooking. Learning to control the fire is a huge part of Kamado cooking success.

I took physics in school and kept telling myself that it was the biggest waste of time because I would never use physics in real life. Well, who knew that there would be physics in grilling! Ha!

"Why did my fire go out?" is probably the most common question I receive. Well, physics would tell us that fire burns up and out in the direction of the fuel, and we already learned that fire needs oxygen to generate combustion. Some of the probing questions I ask in response are: "Did you have enough oxygen for your fire?" "How did you light the fire?" "Did you have enough fuel?" Ninety-five percent of the time, the answer to the original question was that the fire was lit on top of the charcoal, causing the ash to fall on top of the fire and eventually smother it until the point where the fire was suffocated and extinguished. The fire had nowhere to go. The other 5 percent of the answers are typically that the fire ran out of fuel because there was too much fire lit during the initial combustion period.

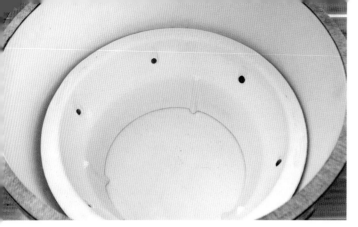

Fire bowl

Kick Ash Basket

Plate setter

Grill grate

FOGO charcoal

Lit fire

Building a fire is fairly simple, but can seem intimidating. As I mentioned earlier, build the fire for the size temperature that you want. When I smoke at 225 to 250°F (110 to 120°C), I start off with a thin layer of FOGO Lump Charcoal or another quality lump charcoal in my Kick Ash Basket. I add two or three wood chunks, followed by another layer of lump and another two or three wood chunks. Layering these wood chunks will ensure that you have a steady amount of smoke throughout your cook. Always fill your charcoal to the top of the basket so that you do not run out of fuel. To light the fire, I dig a well in the charcoal directly above the front air intake vent and place a fire starter there. Remember, fire burns up and out, so make sure you get the coals lit all the way on the bottom of the basket. As the fire burns, the ash will fall through the basket and allow the coal to continue breathing and burning.

Lighting the fire at the edge of the grill directly over the air intake will allow the fire to burn across the diameter of the charcoal. Lighting in the center of the charcoal will cause the fire to burn from the center and out in every direction of the radius of the charcoal. By lighting it at the edge, you will extend, if not double, the length of time of the burn that the charcoal will sustain fire. For example, my XL Big Green Egg, lit at the edge or front of the grill, will burn for nearly 30 hours at 225°F (110°C) with this lighting technique.

Low and slow cooking is all about maintaining a steady, constant temperature, as well as extending the burn of the charcoal as long as possible This will accommodate the larger protein's size. Higher-temperature cooking is not necessarily focused on reserving fuel and typically has a substantially shorter cooking time. When I start a fire for grilling temperatures, I use five fire starters in an XL-sized Big Green Egg: one each at three, six, nine and twelve o'clock and one directly in the center. Remember to get down to the bottom of the charcoal. Lighting in five places will create an even bed of coals and hopefully will generate even grilling temperatures across the entire surface of the grill grate. For a large-sized Big Green Egg, use three fire starters in the shape of a triangle.

Temperature control has a ton to do with the daisy wheel on top of your grill. The Big Green Egg owner's manual tells you to place the daisy wheel on top with the words BIG GREEN EGG facing you. Well, this is terrible advice. Every time you go to open the lid, the swing in the daisy wheel will slide open automatically. Many people forget that happens, walk back inside the house and then wonder why their temperatures have shot up way higher than they want.

My advice is to find your temperature with the daisy wheel. Once you are dialed in, align the two screws on the daisy wheel to line up in a straight perpendicular line with the wooden handle on the dome. Now, when you open the dome, the swing on the daisy wheel hangs right where you left it and does not swing wide open.

Your grill will always perform better when it is clean of ash. I always clean out my grill before a long low and slow cook. I pull the Kick Ash Basket out of the grill and shake it over a galvanized trash can. *Warning: Do not do this with hot lump, coal or ash.* Always make sure that the ash is cool and the fire has gone out. Make sure the air holes in the fire bowl are free from obstruction. Also, pull out the Kick Ash Can and dump out whatever ash is left in the can. If not using the Kick Ash Can, use the stir stick to stir the lump, causing the ash to fall through the grate to be scraped out. Once a year, I pull out the fire ring and bowl and vacuum out everything. A clean grill is a happy grill.

Keeping your grill clean isn't just about removing the ash. Grease drippings and leftover smoking wood need to be cleaned out as well. Any leftover smoking wood might be charred, discolored and difficult to identify after a fire. If you just finished smoking a fatty brisket and are gearing up for a pizza cook, you might decide to dump out the leftover charcoal and start fresh. You might also want to execute a clean burn. Clean burning is conducting a hot 600°F (315°C) burn for about 1 hour. These clean burns are not always required, but they work well to rid the cooker of drippings, wet plate setters and any leftover fire debris.

Did you know that daylight saving time applies to grills? Well it does, sort of. Just like changing out the batteries in your smoke detectors every time you change your clocks, there are certain things that need to be done to your Kamado cooker several times a year, and daylight saving time is when I remember to do it. It just saves me from having to remember when things need to be done. Twice a year, make sure you tighten all the bolts on the cooker's bands. You don't need a torque wrench; just make sure everything is snug so you can avoid a disaster, such as opening the lid and having the dome fall out. It's never happened to me personally, but I've seen it happen to many people. This is also the time that I pull out the fire bowl and ring to clean out any missed ash that could block the airflow.

Cleaning the exterior of a ceramic cooker is not necessary, but many people want it to be clean. Stay away from any harsh cleaners or degreasers. Hot water paired with elbow grease can work wonders. Add some dish soap to your hot water for really dirty spots, then rinse with clean water. This will renew your shine and keep your cooker looking pristine!

These ceramic cookers work perfectly in any and all weather, making them great cookers for our friends in the colder northern climates. Because these cookers retain so much moisture, they are prone to freezing shut, making them useless until they thaw out. If this has happened to you at some point, try placing a layer of waxed paper between the two gaskets. This will keep the two gaskets from freezing together and allow you to use your cooker during any season.

At some point, you will start to see carbon buildup inside the dome of your Kamado cooker as well as in the daisy wheel. If you are doing a lot of low and slow barbecue cooks, you will see this more frequently. Carbon buildup inside a grill is inevitable. However, you do not want that flaky carbon buildup dropping off the dome and onto your food. A good way to combat that hanging carbon is to ball up a large sheet of aluminum foil, wait until the grill is cool and use the ball of foil as a scrubber or use sandpaper to scrub off all the loose hanging carbon. Once your cast-iron daisy wheel gets gunked up and stops turning, toss it on the grill grate during one of your clean burns. Once cool, you can wash it with soap and water, dry it and spray it with some cooking spray to reseason it. All the buildup will be gone and you'll be back in action.

The gaskets on Kamado cookers create a seal between the two halves of the exterior. You won't even notice them when they are working properly. However, you will most definitely notice them when they are worn and not functioning properly. You will see smoke seeping through where the dome and base meet. This is not a problem, but you will lose some of the smoke intended for your proteins. This is an indication that you may have a worn-out gasket that needs to be replaced. Use a putty knife to scrape and remove the old gasket. When the cooker is cool, I use a rag and some acetone to remove any of the sticky residue the old gasket left behind. It takes some effort to get rid of the entire residue, but it is possible. Remove as much as possible before applying the new gasket.

SMOKING BASICS

Smoking is mostly about BBQ. Smoking is generally in the temperature range of 225 to 275°F (110 to 135°C). Larger protein cuts seem to do better with the lower temperature, but cooked with longer times. The low temperature really helps to render the fat in these larger hunks of meat. Some traditional and competition cuts include, but are not limited to, pork shoulder, brisket, ribs, chicken, turkey and sausage.

When I set up my Kamado-style cooker for smoking, I make sure that all of the ash has been cleaned out. Starting with a clean grill will ensure optimum air flow. I add a thin layer of charcoal, then I add three to four chunks of the smoking wood that will be used. Another layer of charcoal, then more smoking wood and so on until the fire bowl is filled. Layering in the smoking wood will ensure even smoke during the entire cook. I dig a well in the coal down to the bottom of the charcoal basket, directly over the bottom air intake, then add a couple of fire starters and light. Because fire burns up and out, lighting at the bottom of the coal will allow the fire to burn up and out, while the ash falls through the fire grate, creating a fire that will last the entire length of your cook. I then add in my diffuser and place the grill grate in place. An optional water pan can be placed at grate level, but is not 100 percent necessary. Once the fire is lit, I close the dome and adjust the bottom vent and daisy wheel close to my cooking temperature. I allow the cooker to come up to cooking temperature slowly. When the cooker gets close to cooking temperature, I start adjusting the bottom vent and daisy wheel to dial in my preferred cooking temperature. Then I get smoking!

GRILLING BASICS

Grilling is typically in the temperature range of 300 to 500°F (148 to 260°C) and is done directly over the coals. I fill my fire bowl completely, open all the vents then add some starter cubes—three in a triangle for a large-sized grill and five in an XL in the center (three, six, nine and twelve o'clock). Then I light them up. The trick to grilling is creating an even coal bed, so placement of the starter cubes is important.

Grilling is generally reserved for smaller items like burgers, steaks, kabobs, chicken breasts, fish and so on. The higher temperature will cook these smaller proteins faster and will require flipping for even cooking.

BAKING BASICS

Yes, your ceramic grill can bake! The trick to baking is to make sure you are cooking with a clean grill. Use the same set-up as you would for smoking, but omit the smoking wood.

The key to baking is to have a smoke-free, clean grill. I try to do a hot burn the day before to clean off any drippings, fat or smoking wood leftover from any previous cooks. Once you are heating your grill to bake, there should be no smoke. When you look at the daisy wheel, you should see a mirage of heat, but zero smoke. If you do have some thin blue smoke, allow the fire to burn for 10 to 15 minutes and it will clear up. If your smoke is clear and you are at your desired cooking temperature, allow the cooker to burn for 30 minutes to preheat all of the ceramic pieces. This is extremely important when using the plate setter and pizza stone. All of the ceramic needs to be hot and ready to cook. An infrared thermometer can help you determine the temperature.

All of this technical talk is making me hungry. Let's light some fires and get smoking!

SMOKING/ BBQ

Barbecue is something that everyone loves to eat and, due to the size of the cuts, brings people together to share in social gatherings. Everyone does it differently, but as long as there is smoke, it is barbecue.

Most barbecue is comprised of proteins cooked using smoke with a minimal amount of other ingredients. Here are some simple yet tasty recipes for you to share at the next barbecue gathering.

THE KING OF TEXAS:
BEEF BRISKET

When discussing brisket, I cannot stress enough how important it is to get a high-quality brisket. In the grand USDA grading system, I will only smoke a Prime or better-graded beef brisket. Sure, I'll still buy a Choice grade if it's pretty marbled, but I will typically grind it into burgers. Fat content is extremely important when cooking brisket. The fat renders as the brisket cooks and basically bastes itself and generates a moist and juicy end result. The one smoked here is a Mishima Reserve Wagyu beef brisket and has a tremendous amount of fat. One thing to keep in mind when smoking a higher-fat-content brisket is that it will take less and less time to finish, based on the grade of the cut. For example, the same weight Choice vs. Prime vs. Wagyu will all finish at different times. A Choice will finish in 16 to 18 hours, the Prime in 12 to 14 and the Wagyu in 8 to 10. It takes a whole lot longer to cook the meat rather than render the fat. A premium-cut brisket will yield a superior end result.

SERVES 8 TO 10

1 whole Prime packer beef brisket (12 to 15 lbs [5.4 to 6.8 kg] on average)

½ cup (120 g) kosher salt

½ cup (51 g) freshly ground black pepper

2 tbsp (18 g) granulated garlic

3 tbsp (16 g) cayenne pepper

5 tbsp (35 g) smoked paprika

PREPARE YOUR BRISKET:

Brisket is the King of BBQ in Texas and seems like one of the hardest cooks for Kamado users. Hopefully, this recipe will make you the king of your briskets. The packer brisket comprises 2 muscles: the flat and the point. The flat, called the "lean" in Texas, is exactly its name and is where brisket slices come from. The point, called the "moist" in Texas, is where burnt ends come from. Both muscles cook completely differently and have their own challenges, but can be very tasty when cooked properly. When selecting a brisket, I prefer a minimum of Prime grade due to the fat content. Anything less than Prime will result in a mediocre brisket, but would be great for ground beef! I also want the thickest flat available to help offset the cooking differences between the 2 muscles. You should also know that the higher the fat content in a brisket, the less time it takes to cook.

I like to trim and season my briskets the night before cooking. I cannot stress how important trimming is when it comes to cooking brisket. The key is to make it aerodynamic. (Physics in barbecue, who knew?!) I start off with the flat muscle facing up. My new preferred trimming blade is a 12-inch (30-cm) slicer. The large blade allows for longer strokes and flatter slices to make the trim a much easier process. I remove every bit of silver skin from the top of the flat.

(CONTINUED)

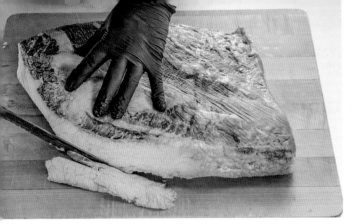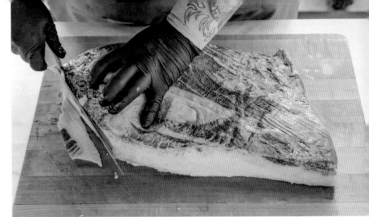

Trimming off the hard fat

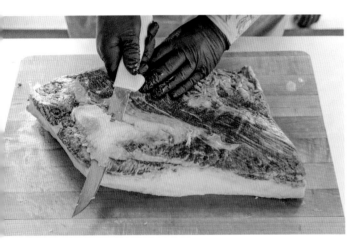

Trimming loose fat and silver skin

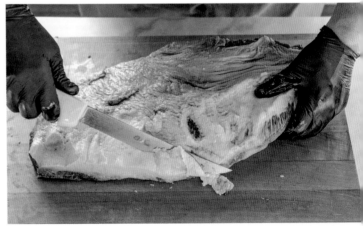

Trimming the bottom fat to ¼ inch (6 mm)

Final trimmed brisket

Bark will set between 160 and 180°F (71 and 82°C).

Time to wrap in butcher paper.

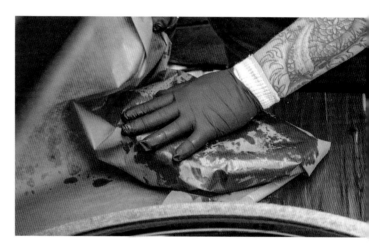

Make sure the wrap is tight.

Slice against the grain. Slices should be as thick as a #2 pencil.

Any straggling pieces get removed as well because they are just going to burn off anyway. The "deckle," the hard piece of fat connecting the 2 muscles, gets trimmed back, but not completely out so as to keep the aerodynamics of the brisket. Now, I flip over the brisket to trim the bottom side. I like to leave about ½ inch (1.3 cm) of fat on this part. That seems like a lot of fat, but I like to use that fat layer as one more barrier of insulation between the brisket and the fire. When all trimmed up, your brisket should be smooth looking without any jagged edges, silver skin or excess hard fat.

In a small bowl, mix together the salt, black pepper, granulated garlic, cayenne and paprika, forming a dry rub, then transfer to a shaker. Don't worry about the cayenne; it won't add any heat, just layers of flavor. Season the brisket liberally. This is a huge chunk of meat, so don't be afraid to add more seasoning. Refrigerate the seasoned brisket overnight.

BIG GREEN EGG SETUP:

Fill your firebox with natural lump charcoal and prepare your Big Green Egg for indirect smoking. Both the daisy wheel and bottom vent should be wide open during ignition. Use a torch or starter cubes to light the charcoal in a single spot to start a bed of coals. Allow the fire to burn for 10 minutes before making any damper adjustments. Add 12 to 15 chunks of smoking wood layered between the charcoal; I like a mix of hickory and cherry with beef brisket. Both the bottom vent and daisy wheel should now be open about 5 percent. The target smoking temperature is about 225°F (110°C) as indicated on your dome thermometer. It is okay if you overshoot the target temperature. Just know that the hotter the fire, the less time will be needed to cook. *This is the one and only cook where I will instruct you to use a water pan.* The water pan creates moisture, which helps create the smoke ring. The Big Green Egg retains enough moisture for other cooks and the water pan is not needed. Place a foil pan on top of the diffuser, fill it with water and place it on top of the grate.

This is the one time that I do not allow the protein to warm to room temperature before adding it to the smoker. Place the cold brisket in the middle of the grill once the smoker is up to temperature. I like to use a wired probe thermometer to keep an eye on the temperature. I check every couple of hours to make sure that there is water in the pan, that the brisket isn't drying out and that there is no pooling of juice or fat forming on the flat because that will ruin the bark in that spot. If you have some pooling, prop up the brisket with a wood chunk to prevent that from happening.

Once the brisket reaches 160°F (71°C), I want to start to look at the bark. I plan on wrapping the brisket, but I want to make sure that the bark is set. This usually happens between 160 and 170°F (71 and 77°C). The bark should not look dry. It should look moist and uniform all over. If it does not look even, allow it to smoke for another 30 minutes and recheck.

WRAP THE BRISKET:

There are two main wrapping materials: foil and butcher paper. It is my opinion that wrapping in foil makes the bark mushy, and that is why I use butcher paper. The butcher paper allows the brisket to breathe, but holds in all the fat and juices of the brisket. I worked at Subway while in high school, so I wrap it like a sub sandwich. I tear off a large sheet of butcher paper, lay it on the diagonal, place the brisket on the paper, fold and flip it over from the top, fold in the left side and flatten the crease, fold in the right side and flatten the crease, flip again and tighten the wrap. The tighter the better, when it comes to wrapping. Even though I flipped the brisket, the flat will still be right side up. Place the brisket back on the smoker and continue to smoke.

Doneness, for me, is not 100 percent about temperature, but more of a feel. Once the wired thermometer registers 200°F (95°C), I like to use my Thermapen as a probe. I probe four or five places all over, looking for tightness. You'll be able to feel any tightness with the probe. If it falls through like butter all over, the brisket is done. If you've got some tight spots, give it another 30 minutes and check again. Some briskets will go all the way up to 205°F (96°C) before they are fully tender.

Once the brisket is tender all over, remove from the smoker and rest in a Cambro hot box, in a cooler or in your oven at 120°F (50°C) for a minimum of 1 hour.

The key to serving brisket is to slice against the grain. You will see the fibrous grain running in one direction. Take your knife and slice the opposite direction, slicing through all of those grains with every slice. Serve in ¼-inch (6-mm)-thick slices.

One note is that I prefer to slice my briskets to order. In other words, I will never slice an entire brisket and allow it to sit out on a cutting board or in a pan for serving. I slice as I serve and leave the remaining brisket intact if everyone has what they want.

SMOKED CHICKEN HALVES

Almost every barbecue restaurant across America serves half chickens. I've had some good and some that are really bad. Each half has both white and dark meat, making it difficult to cook both meats to perfection. Keep the flavors simple and focus on cooking it properly.

SERVES 2

2 tbsp (28 g) kosher salt

1 tbsp (15 g) light brown sugar

1 tbsp (9 g) garlic powder

1 tbsp (7 g) onion powder

1 tbsp (11 g) celery salt

1 tbsp (6 g) freshly ground black pepper

1 tbsp (7 g) smoked paprika

1 tsp cayenne pepper

1 chicken (about 6 lbs [2.7 kg])

½ cup (112 g/1 stick) unsalted butter, sliced

In a small bowl, combine the salt, brown sugar, garlic powder, onion powder, celery salt, black pepper, paprika and cayenne, forming a dry rub. Set aside.

Remove the chicken from its packaging and dry with paper towels. Remove and discard the giblets. Flip the chicken onto its breast so that the backbone is exposed. Cut along each side of the backbone with a pair of kitchen shears, completely removing the backbone. Save that backbone for stock! Flip the bird over to expose the breast. You'll see the breastbone running down the center, giving you the perfect guideline to cut. Use a sharp knife and minimal pressure to slice straight down that line to cut the flesh. This is strictly for cutting the skin so that there are no jagged edges. Follow that same line again with the shears, cutting through the bone to separate the 2 halves. Trim away any excess fat or hanging skin around the neck and thighs, but leave enough to cover the flesh of the chicken.

Flip both halves over so that the carcasses are up. Season the carcasses liberally with the dry rub. Flip the chicken so that the skin side is up. Presentation is key at this point. Pull up each wing and season the outside of the wing. Pull the wing out and back to season the underside. With the wing pulled out of the way, dust the chicken evenly with the rub. Carefully, so as not to disturb the dry rub, place both chicken halves on a baking sheet or in a foil pan and refrigerate for 30 minutes to 1 hour. The salt and spices in the dry rub will pull out any moisture left in the skin, create a natural binder and ensure the rub sticks to the chicken.

(CONTINUED)

SMOKED CHICKEN HALVES (CONTINUED)

BIG GREEN EGG SETUP:

Fill your firebox with natural lump charcoal and prepare your Big Green Egg for indirect smoking. Both the daisy wheel and bottom vent should be wide open during ignition. Use a torch or starter cubes to light the charcoal in a single spot to start a bed of coals. Allow the fire to burn for 10 minutes before making any damper adjustments. Add 5 or 6 chunks of smoking wood layered between the charcoal; I like pecan wood with poultry. Both the bottom vent and daisy wheel should now be open about 10 percent. The target smoking temperature is about 250°F (120°C) as indicated on your dome thermometer. It is okay if you overshoot the target temperature. Just know that the hotter the fire, the less time will be needed to cook.

Once the smoker is up to temperature, carefully place the 2 chicken halves in the center of the grill. Using a wire thermometer, smoke the chicken until it reaches 130°F (55°C). At that point, place the 2 chicken halves in a pan. Place the pats of butter on top of the chicken, then place the pan back onto the smoker. The butter will melt and baste the chicken. Baste every 15 to 20 minutes by dipping a brush or mop into the butter and drizzling it over top until the internal temperature of the breast hits 160°F (71°C). Remove the chicken from the smoker and serve immediately.

TEXAS-STYLE SMOKED TURKEY BREAST

Very few barbecue restaurants are nailing Texas-style smoked turkey breast. It is so simple yet hard to keep the moisture in the breast. One trick is the butter-poach method, which is what I prefer to use. A quick brine might help as well.

SERVES 6 TO 8

1 whole fresh bone-in turkey breast (3 to 3½ lbs [1.4 to 1.6 kg])

1 tbsp (15 g) kosher salt

2 tbsp (13 g) coarsely ground black pepper

1 cup (225 g/2 sticks) unsalted butter

BIG GREEN EGG SETUP:

Fill your firebox with natural lump charcoal and prepare your Big Green Egg for indirect smoking. Both the daisy wheel and bottom vent should be wide open during ignition. Use a torch or starter cubes to light the charcoal in a single spot to start a bed of coals. Allow the fire to burn for 10 minutes before making any damper adjustments. Add 5 or 6 chunks of smoking wood layered between the charcoal; I like pecan wood with turkey. Both the bottom vent and daisy wheel should now be open about 10 percent. The target smoking temperature is about 250°F (120°C) as indicated on your dome thermometer. It is okay if you overshoot the target temperature. Just know that the hotter the fire, the less time will be needed to cook.

Low and slow barbecue requires low temperatures to render all the fat out of the larger cuts. Brisket and pork are best at around the 225°F (110°C) smoking temperature. Poultry has very little fat, so cooking at a slightly higher temperature is perfectly acceptable.

Remove the turkey breast from its packaging and dry with paper towels. Use your fingers to get in under the skin and carefully remove the skin from the breast. Using a boning knife, remove the flesh from the carcass. Using small, short slices against the rib cage will maximize the amount of flesh that can be removed from the carcass. Always save the skin and carcass to make stock!

In a shaker, mix together the salt and pepper. I actually keep a full shaker of a 1-to-2 ratio of kosher salt and pepper on hand in my pantry for all my Texas barbecue proteins. Dust the turkey breast with an even coating of the salt and pepper mixture. Place the turkey breast, smooth side up, in the center of the grill for a smoke bath.

(CONTINUED)

TEXAS-STYLE SMOKED TURKEY BREAST (CONTINUED)

I like to monitor my indirect cooks with a wire thermometer. Smoke the turkey breast until it hits 110°F (45°C). Remove the turkey breast from the smoker. Lay out 2 sheets of aluminum foil for each breast on a work surface and place the turkey breast, smooth side down, on the foil. Slice the sticks of butter in half lengthwise and place 2 halves on top of each breast. Pull the opposite sides of the foil up and together and roll tight. Roll each end in a similar fashion to create an airtight packet. Place the foil packet back on the smoker. The foil packet with the butter inside will create a poaching environment. Poaching will allow the protein to cook at a slow temperature without losing its moisture, making the turkey tender, juicy and succulent.

Continue to smoke the turkey until it hits an internal temperature of 160°F (71°C). Allow the turkey to rest in a Cambro hot box, cooler or 120°F (50°C) oven for a minimum of 45 minutes.

Carefully open the foil pouch and allow the steam to release. Remove the turkey breast and allow the poaching butter to drain. Slice into thin slices to serve.

PORK SHOULDER (BOSTON BUTT) & SLAW

One of the easiest and tastiest pieces of barbecue is a pork shoulder, also known as a Boston butt. This cut comes from the shoulder of the pig and usually averages 8 to 10 pounds (3.6 to 4.5 kg). When selecting one in a store, you want to select a bone-in butt. The bone will aid in achieving a more even cook, and the meat around a bone is always better!

SERVES 8 TO 10, DEPENDING ON SIZE

1 bone-in Boston butt (usually 8 to 10 lbs [3.6 to 4.5 kg])

½ cup (120 g) kosher salt

5 tbsp (35 g) smoked paprika

3 tbsp (19 g) freshly ground black pepper

1 tsp onion powder

1 tsp garlic powder

1 tsp cayenne pepper

½ cup (115 g) light brown sugar

1 tsp mustard powder

1 tsp chili powder

½ tsp ground cumin

½ cup (120 ml) apple juice

¼ cup (60 ml) bourbon (whatever I'm drinking at the time)

BIG GREEN EGG SETUP:

Fill your firebox with natural lump charcoal and prepare your Big Green Egg for indirect smoking. Both the daisy wheel and bottom vent should be wide open during ignition. Use a torch or starter cubes to light the charcoal in a single spot to start a bed of coals. Allow the fire to burn for 10 minutes before making any damper adjustments. Add 5 or 6 chunks of smoking wood layered between the charcoal; I like apple wood with pork. Both the bottom vent and daisy wheel should now be open about 5 percent. The target smoking temperature is about 225°F (110°C) as indicated on your dome thermometer. It is okay if you overshoot the target temperature. Just know that the hotter the fire, the less time will be needed to cook.

Remove the Boston butt from its packaging and pat dry with paper towels. I prefer to trim off the fat cap as much as possible to increase the amount of bark that will form. There is plenty of fat running through the shoulder that will self-baste the pork throughout the cook, so removing the fat cap is no big deal.

In a small bowl, whisk together the salt, paprika, black pepper, onion powder, garlic powder, cayenne, brown sugar, mustard powder, chili powder and cumin, forming a dry rub. Cover the pork shoulder liberally with the dry rub. This is a large cut of meat, so don't get concerned that there is too much seasoning. Reserve any dry rub that is not used for later.

Place the pork shoulder in the center of the grill grate once the grill has preheated and smoke is rolling from the daisy wheel. I like to monitor the shoulder with a wired thermometer with Wi-Fi capabilities. This cook will most likely take 12+ hours, so the Wi-Fi thermometer allows me to monitor the cook without being tied to the grill all day.

(CONTINUED)

Trim the fat cap off . . .

. . . Final trim of the pork butt

Check the internal temperature to make sure it's done.

The bone should pull out clean.

SLAW

1 head green cabbage (about 2 lbs [905 g]), shredded

½ head red cabbage (about 1 lb [455 g]), shredded

4 carrots, peeled and shredded

2 bunches green onions, sliced on the bias

¼ cup (60 ml) mayonnaise (Duke's is the only real mayo)

2 tbsp (30 ml) cider vinegar

1 tbsp (18 g) salt

1 tbsp (6 g) freshly ground black pepper

½ tsp cayenne pepper

I like to start checking on the progress around 3 hours into the cook. I want to make sure that the bark is not drying out. In a spray bottle, mix the apple juice and bourbon together and use that to spritz the pork when it needs some moisture. Once the pork reaches an internal temperature of 175°F (79°C), I like to wrap the Boston butt. I place a double layer of wide heavy-duty foil on the counter, set the butt on it, pull the corners up so that I can add a small bit of the spritz liquid inside the foil, then wrap it up tightly. Place the Boston butt back on the grill.

Once the shoulder reaches an internal temperature of 195°F (91°C), I like to start checking for tenderness. I use the probe of my Thermapen to check 4 or 5 different spots for any tightness in the shoulder. If the probe slides in and out easily, the shoulder is done. If there is some tightness, allow the shoulder to smoke for another 30 minutes and try again, repeating this step as many times as necessary.

Rest the shoulder in a Cambro hot box, cooler or oven at 120°F (50°C) for a minimum of 1 hour.

Remove the shoulder from the foil and pull it apart with your hands. I like to use cotton gloves under nitrile gloves to help handle the hot pork. As I pull the pork, I dust it with some of the leftover dry rub.

PREPARE THE SLAW:

In a large bowl, mix together all the ingredients. Refrigerate for a minimum of 1 hour before serving. Serve on top of the pork on a sandwich or as a side.

MEAT CANDY
(A.K.A. PORK RIBS)

I like my ribs to be sweet and sticky. There are two types of ribs: spare and baby back, and several different cuts of ribs to choose from full spare, St. Louis cut and full baby back. The St. Louis cut spare rib, the most common style in competition barbecue, has all the fringe and cartilage trimmed off. When selecting a rack of ribs, you want to try to pick a rack that has heavy marbling, straight bones and as few shiners as possible. (Shiners are places in the rack where the butcher has cut down into the bones.)

SERVES 4

2 (2½-lb [1.1-kg]) racks
St. Louis–style spare ribs

Ribs are one of my all-time favorite things to cook. They are sweet and sticky and come with a built-in handle! There are a couple of things to look for when selecting your racks of ribs. I prefer racks that are thick and heavily marbled. Fat is flavor, so I want as much of it as I can get. Also, skip over racks with "shiners." They are hard to see on the underneath side, but do your best at looking at the meat side.

Now that the proper ribs have been selected, it's time to prep them. Ribs have a silver skin or membrane on the underneath side of the bones that needs to be removed. Some heavy-volume restaurants leave this membrane on as a time saver, but I assure you that no one wants to eat that. Use the handle end of a spoon or a butter knife to loosen up some of the membrane from the protein so that you can get your finger under it. Work your finger under and pull the membrane away from the bones and ultimately off the ribs altogether. Some people will use a paper towel for a better grip; I sometimes will add a pinch of the dry rub I'd be using on the ribs for some extra texture on that membrane to help me pull it off. There should be a minimal amount of trimming on ribs. Trim off any loose pieces that will burn off anyway. I also like to square them up a bit to help them cook evenly.

(CONTINUED)

Trim any loose pieces of meat.

Use a spoon handle or butter knife to get under the membrane to loosen it.

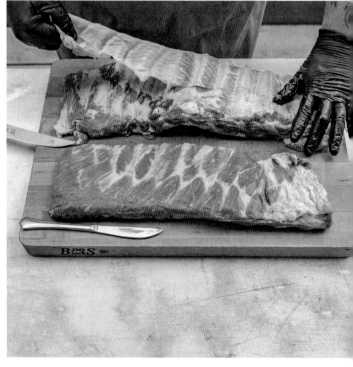

Peel back the membrane and discard.

Trim any loose ends.

The final trim.

Cook it up . . .

. . . and slice.

MEAT CANDY (CONTINUED)

½ cup (120 g) kosher salt

5 tbsp (35 g) smoked paprika

3 tbsp (19 g) freshly ground black pepper

1 tsp onion powder

1 tsp garlic powder

1 tsp cayenne pepper

½ cup (115 g) light brown sugar

1 tsp mustard powder

1 tsp chili powder

½ tsp ground cumin

½ cup (120 ml) apple juice

¼ cup (60 ml) bourbon (whatever I am drinking at the time)

¼ cup (60 ml) honey

½ cup (112 g/1 stick) unsalted butter

1 cup (240 ml) Gentry's Tenne-Sweet BBQ Sauce

In a small bowl, whisk together the salt, paprika, black pepper, onion powder, garlic powder, cayenne, brown sugar, mustard powder, chili powder and cumin, forming a dry rub. I do not use a binder for my dry rub, so save all that yellow mustard for your sandwiches. Dust a layer of the dry rub over the ribs, starting with the bones side first, then the meat side. Seasoning the bones side first will keep the rub from falling off the meat side when you flip them. Allow the ribs to sit at room temperature for 30 minutes. During this time, the seasoning will make the meat sweat and create a natural binder to adhere the rub.

BIG GREEN EGG SETUP:

While the ribs rest, fill your firebox with natural lump charcoal and prepare your Big Green Egg for indirect smoking. Both the daisy wheel and bottom vent should be wide open during ignition. Use a torch or starter cubes to light the charcoal in a single spot to start a bed of coals. Allow the fire to burn for 10 minutes before making any damper adjustments. Add 5 or 6 chunks of smoking wood layered between the charcoal; I like apple wood with pork. Both the bottom vent and daisy wheel should now be open about 5 percent. The target smoking temperature is about 225°F (110°C) as indicated on your dome thermometer. It is okay if you overshoot the target temperature. Just know that the hotter the fire, the less time will be needed to cook.

Place the ribs in the center of the grill grate. In a spray bottle, combine the apple juice and bourbon and use that to spritz the ribs every 30 minutes. Each time I spritz, I am looking for a light mahogany color to the ribs before I wrap them. The right color is typically somewhere in the 2- to 2½-hour mark.

WRAP THE RIBS:

Once I get the correct color, I remove the ribs from the grill. For each rack of ribs, spread out a layer of wide heavy-duty aluminum foil. Drizzle a layer of honey onto an area of the foil roughly the size of the rack of ribs, place 2 pats of butter down on the foil, then place the ribs, meat side down, on the foil. Repeat the honey and butter on the bone side of the ribs. The trick to wrapping is getting the foil wrapped tight. Take both sides of foil and bring them up over the rack of ribs. Roll the 2 sides together to create a tight seal. Crumple each end and roll the same way. This will create an airtight pouch and allow the ribs to steam inside the foil, making them ultratender. Smoke for 1 hour and check for tenderness. Put the Gentry's Tenne-Sweet BBQ Sauce in a grillproof saucepan and place on the grill.

Remove the foil pouches from the grill. Carefully open the foil and allow the steam to release before opening completely. Unroll and open the foil. The honey and butter should be melted and the meat should have drawn away from the bones. Slightly twist a couple of the bones to see if they are loose. If not, wrap the foil back up and cook for another 20 to 30 minutes. The internal temperature needs to be 190°F (88°C). If the rib meat feels tender and the internal temperature is close, remove the ribs from the foil pouches and allow the liquid to drain off the ribs. Apply the Gentry's Tenne-Sweet BBQ Sauce with a brush. Always warm a glaze prior to application to ensure a smooth, unclumpy glaze. The brushstrokes should go the same direction as the bones. If you've ever seen *The Karate Kid* movie, you want to paint the fence, not the house. Brushstrokes in the same direction as the bones, with a warm glaze, will eliminate any brushstrokes from your presentation.

Smoke for another 20 to 30 minutes to set the glaze. Remove the ribs from the smoker once the glaze is tacky. Slice to serve.

THINGS ON A STICK

Several years ago, a friend of mine made a comment about a beef rib: "This is like brisket on a stick!" Instantly, the comment stuck, and now anything that's on a bone or skewer has been referred as "on a stick". Here are some of my favorite things on "sticks" for you to enjoy.

SMO-FRIED WINGS
WITH HABANERO BBQ SAUCE

There is nothing better than the texture of something fried. Why not add some smoke flavor as well?! This combination is my absolute favorite when it comes to chicken wings. I will give a disclaimer when it comes to frying over an open flame. Please be careful and exercise common sense when doing this. Do your best not to drip any of the oil down into the fire, to avoid flare-ups.

SERVES 2

1 dozen chicken wings separated into drums and flats

Extra virgin olive oil

Salt and freshly ground black pepper

½ Vidalia onion, minced

2 habanero peppers, minced, seeds included

1 clove garlic, minced

2 tbsp (30 ml) of whatever bourbon you are drinking

¾ cup (175 ml) ketchup

⅓ cup (80 ml) cider vinegar

1 tbsp (15 ml) Worcestershire sauce

¼ cup (60 ml) honey

3 tbsp (45 ml) hot sauce

¼ tsp freshly grated nutmeg

Peanut oil, for frying

BIG GREEN EGG SETUP:

Fill your firebox with natural lump charcoal and prepare your Big Green Egg for indirect smoking. Both the daisy wheel and bottom vent should be wide open during ignition. Use a torch or starter cubes to light the charcoal in a single spot to start a bed of coals. Allow the fire to burn for 10 minutes before making any damper adjustments. Add 4 or 5 chunks of smoking wood; I like pecan with chicken. Both the bottom vent and daisy wheel should now be open about 10 percent. The target smoking temperature is about 275°F (135°C) as indicated on your dome thermometer. It is okay if you overshoot the target temperature. Just know that the hotter the fire, the less time will be needed to cook.

Rinse your chicken wings under cold running water and then dry them thoroughly with paper towels. Place them in a mixing bowl, drizzle in some olive oil, add a couple of pinches of salt and pepper and toss the wings around to coat them evenly. Place them on a clean grill grate for a smoke bath. Wings, depending on size, will need to smoke for about 1 hour.

While the wings are smoking, make the habanero barbecue sauce: Heat a medium saucepan over medium heat. Drizzle in 2 tablespoons (30 ml) of olive oil and add the onion and habanero peppers. Sweat these down for about 5 minutes to take off their raw edge. Add the minced garlic to the saucepan and continue to sweat until the garlic has softened and has become fragrant. Splash in the bourbon and cook for about 3 minutes to burn off the alcohol. Add the ketchup, vinegar, Worcestershire, honey, hot sauce and nutmeg to the saucepan, bring to a boil, then lower the heat to low. Cover and simmer for about 30 minutes. Always taste for salt and pepper and adjust accordingly.

(CONTINUED)

SMO-FRIED WINGS (CONTINUED)

Fill a Dutch oven with 1½ inches (4 cm) of peanut oil. Place over medium heat and bring the oil to 350°F (180°C).

Once the wings have reached an internal temperature of 170°F (77°C), remove them from the smoker and place on paper towels to absorb any juices or liquid. Slowly drop 4 wings at a time into the hot oil and fry for about 3 minutes, or until crispy. Remove them from the oil and allow them to drain on paper towels. Once all of the wings have been fried, place them in a large bowl, drizzle some of the habanero barbecue sauce over them and toss to coat evenly.

There's nothing better than the crunchiness of a fried wing, with the smoke flavor from the smoker and a sweet/heat barbecue sauce to lick off your fingers.

NOTE: Yes, you can fry on the grill. However, you must exercise extreme caution when doing so. Use a deep Dutch oven and make sure your fire is a bed of coals rather than a roaring fire. I typically fry on the grill to prevent my house from smelling like McDonald's.

DRY-BRINED TOMAHAWK RIB EYE
WITH COMPOUND BUTTER

One of my favorite cuts of beef is a tomahawk rib eye. They are just massive! I like to cook it for friends and family because they are always impressed.

SERVES 2 OR 3

1 tomahawk prime grade rib eye (typically 48 to 60 oz [1.4 to 1.7 kg])

Kosher salt

1 tbsp (15 ml) extra virgin olive oil

Freshly ground black pepper

¼ cup (55 g/½ stick) unsalted butter, at room temperature

1 tbsp (10 g) grated fresh garlic (use a Microplane)

1 tbsp (3 g) finely chopped fresh chives

1 tbsp (10 g) grated shallot (use a Microplane)

¼ tsp cayenne pepper

I like to dry brine any superthick steaks. This tomahawk rib eye is nearly 3 inches (7.5 cm) thick and will lack flavor on the inside without dry brining. Apply a decent amount of kosher salt over the entire surface of the steak, place on a wire rack set upon a baking sheet and refrigerate, uncovered, overnight. The salt will melt and penetrate into the steak, creating flavor all the way to the center, while ejecting some of the wet aging agent used by the processor. Both of these are good things. The tomahawk will have an almost dry aged look to it with a deeper red color than the day before.

Remove the steak from the refrigerator for a minimum of 1 hour prior to cooking. Brush the olive oil on the steak and dust with black pepper.

BIG GREEN EGG SETUP:

Fill your firebox with natural lump charcoal and prepare your Big Green Egg for indirect smoking. Both the daisy wheel and bottom vent should be wide open during ignition. Use a torch or starter cubes to light the charcoal in a single spot to start a bed of coals. Allow the fire to burn for 10 minutes before making any damper adjustments. Add 4 or 5 chunks of smoking wood; I like hickory with steak. Both the bottom vent and daisy wheel should now be open about 10 percent. The target smoking temperature is about 250°F (120°C) as indicated on your dome thermometer. It is okay if you overshoot the target temperature. Just know that the hotter the fire, the less time will be needed to cook.

Once the grill has preheated to your smoking temperature, add the steak. Slow smoking the steak first will generate great smokey flavor as well as provide a perfect cooked temperature throughout the entire steak. I prefer my steak medium-rare, so I smoke mine to 130°F (54°C), which is less than the final target temperature, but that's okay because there will be some carryover cooking and a high-heat sear after to get to the correct temperature.

(CONTINUED)

DRY-BRINED TOMAHAWK RIB EYE (CONTINUED)

Here are the temperature ranges for those with different preferences:

Rare: 125°F (52°C)—cool red center

Medium-rare: 135°F (57°C)—warm red center

Medium: 145°F (63°C)—warm pink center

Medium-well: 150°F (66°C)—slightly pink center

Well-done: 160°F (71°C) plus—zero pink center

While the steak is smoking, let's make a tasty compound butter to finish our meal. In a medium bowl, combine the butter, garlic, chives, shallot, cayenne and salt and black pepper to taste. A fork is my mixing utensil of choice. Make sure the mixture is thoroughly blended. Lay out a sheet of plastic wrap on the counter and dump the butter mixture onto the center of the plastic wrap. Fold over one side of the plastic wrap and use it to roll the butter mixture into a log. Then, twist both ends like a giant Tootsie Roll. Place in the refrigerator while we wait on our steak.

Once the steak has reached your desired internal temperature, remove it from the smoke and transfer it to a plate or baking sheet. Don't cover or tent the steak with foil, or it will continue to cook. At this point, put on your insulated grilling gloves and remove the grill diffuser, changing the grilling setup from indirect to direct. Open the vent and the daisy wheel and increase the grilling temperature to 600°F (315°C). This should take about 10 minutes.

Before you sear the tomahawk, wrap the bone in foil. You spent a ton of money on this premium steak, and wrapping the bone in foil will ensure a beautiful presentation.

When the grill is ready to sear the steak, my preferred method is to use a timer. Without a timer, you will end up with one side of your steak overcooked, every time. So start with 1 minute per side, assess the crust, then adjust by adding 30 seconds at a time to each side, a total of 2 minutes per side max. Remove the steak from the high heat, top with a couple of slices of the compound butter and tent the steak loosely with foil. Resting the steak 10 minutes prior to slicing will allow the butter to melt, releasing all those great flavors, and will allow all the juices to slow down inside the steak and distribute evenly throughout. Slice to serve.

RACK OF LAMB
WITH RED WINE REDUCTION

Rack of lamb is an expensive cut for most folks. I hear a lot from people that they are scared they will ruin it. Here's the fail-safe way to cook it. Lamb does well with garlic, fresh herbs and a simple seasoning of salt and pepper.

SERVES 2

1 tsp extra virgin olive oil

4 shallots, roughly chopped

1 clove garlic, minced

1 cup (240 ml) dark red wine (something drinkable)

2 cups (475 ml) beef stock

2 sprigs thyme

1 sprig rosemary

1 tbsp (15 ml) water

Salt and freshly ground black pepper

1 tbsp (14 g) unsalted butter

1 (8-bone) rack of lamb

Pinch of Italian seasoning

BIG GREEN EGG SETUP:

Fill your firebox with natural lump charcoal and prepare your Big Green Egg for direct grilling. The target grilling temperature is about 450°F (230°C) as indicated on your dome thermometer. You want to create a mature fire with no flame. If you allow your Big Green Egg to burn at its target temperature, in this case 450°F (230°C), for at least 10 minutes, all the lit coals should be glowing orange without a flame—this is an indication that you have built a mature fire.

Heat a large skillet over medium heat on the stovetop. Add the olive oil and sauté the shallots and garlic until they are fragrant. Deglaze the skillet with the wine and bring to a boil. Add the beef stock, thyme, rosemary, water and salt and pepper to taste. Bring the mixture back to a boil and then lower the heat to a simmer. Allow the mixture to reduce down to about 1 tablespoon (15 ml). Remove from the heat, strain through a sieve and return to the skillet. Without any heat, drop the butter into the skillet and swirl the butter into the reduction. Simply swirl the skillet in a circle until the butter melts into the reduction to make a sauce.

Season the lamb with a generous sprinkle of salt, pepper and a pinch of Italian seasoning. Grill it over a direct flame until the internal temperature reaches 130°F (54°C), approximately 12 to 15 minutes. When I grill anything with a bone, I like to hang the bones out of the grill so they do not get charred.

Rest the lamb for a minimum of 6 minutes before slicing and plating. Serve with the sauce.

BEEF PLATE RIBS
(BRISKET ON A STICK)

We've all watched an episode or two of *The Flintstones* cartoons. The most famous or well-known clip is the intro where a waitress brings out a massive cut of dinosaur meat. Ha! That is what I always think about when I cook these huge beef ribs. *Willllllmmaaaa!!!!*

SERVES 4 OR 5

6 lbs (2.7 kg) 3-bone beef plate rib

3 to 4 tbsp (45 to 60 ml) hot sauce (I like Cholula or Tabasco)

2 tbsp (36 g) salt

2 tbsp (13 g) freshly ground black pepper

1 cup (240 ml) beef stock, as needed

BIG GREEN EGG SETUP:

Fill your firebox with natural lump charcoal and prepare your Big Green Egg for indirect smoking. Both the daisy wheel and bottom vent should be wide open during ignition. Use a torch or starter cubes to light the charcoal in a single spot to start a bed of coals. Allow the fire to burn for 10 minutes before making any damper adjustments. Add 4 to 5 chunks of smoking wood; I like hickory with steak. Both the bottom vent and daisy wheel should now be open about 15 percent. The target smoking temperature is about 275°F (135°C) as indicated on your dome thermometer. It is okay if you overshoot the target temperature. Just know that the hotter the fire, the less time will be needed to cook.

Trim some of the fat off the ribs, but don't get crazy with it. You'll want to keep some of the fat on them. I like to slather my beef ribs with a binder to get the seasoning to stick, and hot sauce is my favorite binder. Slather the hot sauce all over the ribs and dust with salt and pepper. Allow the beef ribs to come to room temperature for about an hour. Once the grill is preheated, place the ribs into the center of the grill.

These ribs will take about 5 hours to cook. I like to start looking at the bark at around the 2-hour mark. If you start to see dry spots on the bark, use a spray bottle to spritz them with the beef stock to add moisture. Continue checking every hour and spritz as necessary.

Smoke the ribs to an internal temperature of 205°F (96°C). Remove them from the smoker and place them in a Cambro hot box, a cooler or an oven preheated to 120°F (50°C) to hold them. They should rest for about 45 minutes before serving. These ribs are supereasy, ultrarich and very tasty.

SRIRACHA PEACH-GLAZED PORK CHOPS

I'm from Georgia, y'all, so there has to be some sort of peach recipe!

SERVES 2

¼ cup (50 g) sugar

¼ cup (60 g) kosher salt

4 cups (946 ml) water

2 double-cut pork chops (generally 12 to 14 oz [340 to 400 g])

Olive oil, for brushing

GLAZE

1 cup (320 g) peach preserves

2 tbsp (30 ml) sriracha

2 tbsp (30 g) light brown sugar

¼ tsp cayenne pepper

½ tsp ground cinnamon

½ tsp garlic powder

RUB

¼ cup (60 g) light brown sugar

1 tbsp (6 g) freshly ground black pepper

½ tsp smoked paprika

¼ tsp cayenne pepper

1 tbsp (15 g) kosher salt

½ tsp garlic powder

½ tsp onion powder

In a medium bowl, combine the sugar, salt and water. Whisk vigorously. The water will get cloudy, but continue to whisk until the water becomes clear. The clear water is an indication that the sugar and salt have dissolved. Place the pork chops in a ziplock bag, cover with the brine mixture and refrigerate for 24 hours.

BIG GREEN EGG SETUP:

Fill your firebox with natural lump charcoal and prepare your Big Green Egg for direct grilling. The target grilling temperature is about 400°F (200°C) as indicated on your dome thermometer. Both the bottom vent and daisy wheel should be open about 40 percent, but small adjustments might be required. You want to create a mature fire with no flame. If you allow your Big Green Egg to burn at its target temperature, in this case 400°F (200°C), for at least 10 minutes, all the lit coals should be glowing orange without a flame—this is an indication that you have built a mature fire.

PREPARE THE GLAZE:

In a saucepan, combine all the glaze ingredients. Warm the glaze on low heat to melt the preserves. Keep the glaze warm until ready to use.

PREPARE THE RUB:

In a small bowl, combine all the rub ingredients.

Remove the pork chops from the brine and pat dry with paper towels. Brush the chops with olive oil and season with the rub. Place in the center of the hot grill. This rub has sugar in it, so keep the chops moving on the grill to avoid unnecessary charring.

Once you have achieved some grill marks and some char, start applying the glaze. Apply the glaze each time you flip the chop. Grill the pork chops to an internal temperature of 137°F (58°C). Let rest for 8 to 10 minutes prior to serving.

BRAISED LAMB SHANKS

Lamb shanks are one of my favorite comfort foods and are great in wintertime to warm you up on a cold night.

SERVES 4

4 lamb shanks (generally 12 to 14 oz [340 to 400 g] each)

Salt and freshly ground black pepper

3 tbsp (45 ml) extra virgin olive oil

3 tbsp (42 g) unsalted butter, divided

½ yellow onion, diced

2 celery ribs, diced

1 large carrot, diced

4 cloves garlic, minced

2 tbsp (15 g) all-purpose flour

1 cup (240 ml) red wine

3 cups (710 ml) chicken stock

½ cup (120 ml) water

3 sprigs rosemary

5 sprigs thyme

Mashed potatoes, for serving

BIG GREEN EGG SETUP:

Fill your firebox with natural lump charcoal and prepare your Big Green Egg for indirect roasting. Both the daisy wheel and bottom vent should be wide open during ignition. Use a torch or starter cubes to light the charcoal in a single spot to start a bed of coals. Allow the fire to burn for 10 minutes before making any damper adjustments. I do not add any smoking wood. Both the bottom vent and daisy wheel should now be open about 30 percent. The target smoking temperature is about 350°F (180°C) as indicated on your dome thermometer. It is okay if you overshoot the target temperature. Just know that the hotter the fire, the less time will be needed to cook.

Heat a 6-quart (5.7-L) Dutch oven on the grill for 15 minutes. While the Dutch oven heats, season the lamb shanks with salt and pepper. Drizzle the extra virgin olive oil into the Dutch oven. Place the lamb shanks in the Dutch oven and allow the exterior to caramelize. Don't worry about overcooking them; they would need a lot more time than the few minutes that they are searing. Turn and sear them until they are golden brown all the way around. This takes about 3 minutes per side. Once browned, remove the shanks from the Dutch oven and cover them with foil.

Mirepoix is French for "onion, celery and carrot." Add 2 tablespoons (28 g) of the butter and the mirepoix to the Dutch oven, and season with salt and pepper. Continually stir until the vegetables are soft and browned. This is one of the times that we are looking for browned veggies because they will add flavor to the braising liquid, which will turn into the sauce. Once browned, add the garlic and flour. Stir until every bit of vegetable is covered with flour and the garlic starts to become fragrant. Then, stir in the red wine, chicken stock and water. Drop in the rosemary, the thyme and then the shanks. The shanks should be covered three-quarters of the way up with the liquid. If not, add more stock and water. Season with salt and pepper, cover and allow to braise for 2 hours. The shanks should be fork tender, but firm enough to still hold onto the bone. If they are, remove the Dutch oven from the heat. Carefully remove the shanks from the liquid, cover with foil and set aside. Strain the braising liquid through a strainer to remove the herbs and veggies. Place the Dutch oven on the grill, add the liquid back into the Dutch oven, bring to a boil and allow to reduce for 10 minutes. Spoon off the foaming fat while it boils. Once reduced to a thick sauce and *nappe* (French for the "sauce is thick enough to coat the back of a spoon"), turn off the heat, drop in the last tablespoon (14 g) of butter and swirl with a wooden spoon or a spatula. Do not use a whisk! A whisk will thin the sauce. Taste for salt and pepper and adjust. Plate the shanks over top of mashed potatoes, then spoon the beautiful pan sauce over everything.

STEAK KEBABS
WITH CHINESE GARLIC SAUCE

Man has been skewering meat for centuries. Kebabs can be whatever you'd like them to be, but they typically consist of some sort of protein on a wooden stick cooked over fire. Kebabs can be dry rubbed, marinated or sauced. The world is your oyster when it comes to kebabs.

SERVES 2

1 (1-lb [455-g]) rib eye

1 sweet onion

1 green bell pepper

6 to 8 oz (170 to 225 g) cherry tomatoes

Extra virgin olive oil

Salt and freshly ground black pepper

CHINESE GARLIC SAUCE

2 tbsp (30 ml) rice vinegar

2 tbsp (26 g) sugar

1 tbsp (15 ml) soy sauce

2 tbsp (30 ml) honey

1 tbsp (15 ml) molasses

1 tsp Worcestershire sauce

2 tsp (10 ml) Chinese rice wine

½ tsp gochujang

¼ tsp sesame oil

1 tbsp (15 ml) canola oil

4 cloves garlic, finely grated (use a Microplane)

Have ready 5 or 6 skewers. If you are using wooden skewers, soak them in water for 20 minutes prior to grilling. This will slow the char and burning of the wood.

BIG GREEN EGG SETUP:

Fill your firebox with natural lump charcoal and prepare your Big Green Egg for direct grilling. The target grilling temperature is about 425°F (220°C) as indicated on your dome thermometer. Both the bottom vent and daisy wheel should be open about 50 percent, but small adjustments might be required. You want to create a mature fire with no flame. If you allow your Big Green Egg to burn at its target temperature, in this case 425°F (220°C), for at least 10 minutes, all the lit coals should be glowing orange without a flame—this is your indication that you have built a mature fire.

Cut the rib eye, onion and bell pepper into cubes. Thread the steak, onion and pepper cubes and the tomatoes onto skewers. Brush the kebabs with extra virgin olive oil and season all sides with salt and black pepper. Set aside until ready to grill.

PREPARE THE CHINESE GARLIC SAUCE:

In a small bowl, combine all the sauce ingredients and whisk thoroughly. Set aside until ready to grill.

Place the kebabs in the middle of the hot grill. Cook, rotating every 2 minutes. Once the kebabs have been grilled all the way around, brush with the Chinese garlic sauce and repeat, grilling on each side until the steak reaches an internal temperature of 135°F (57°C).

DISNEY-STYLE TURKEY LEG

While I was growing up in the midwestern United States, my family always took the vacations that midwesterners take: a trip to see the Mouse. I'm talking about Disney World. There are two specific food items that bring back memories for me: a Mouseketeer Bar and Disney World's world-famous turkey legs. And seeing as how this is a grilling book, I won't be able to grill a Mouseketeer Bar. Ha!

SERVES 4

1 cup (200 g) sugar

1 cup (240 g) kosher salt

1 gallon (3.8 L) water

4 turkey legs

¼ cup (48 g) Code 3 Spices Garlic Grunt Rub

In a bowl, combine the sugar, salt and water and whisk. The water will start out cloudy, but keep whisking until the water becomes clear. Drop the turkey legs into the water and refrigerate for 48 hours. This brine will cure the turkey legs similarly to the legs they serve at all Disney theme parks.

BIG GREEN EGG SETUP:

Fill your firebox with natural lump charcoal and prepare your Big Green Egg for indirect smoking. Both the daisy wheel and bottom vent should be wide open during ignition. Use a torch or starter cubes to light the charcoal in a single spot to start a bed of coals. Allow the fire to burn for 10 minutes before making any damper adjustments. Add 5 or 6 chunks of smoking wood layered between the charcoal; I like pecan wood with turkey. Both the bottom vent and daisy wheel should now be open about 10 percent. The target smoking temperature is about 250°F (120°C) as indicated on your dome thermometer. It is okay if you overshoot the target temperature. Just know that the hotter the fire, the less time will be needed to cook.

Remove the legs from the brine, pat dry with paper towels and discard the brine. Season the turkey legs with Code 3 Spices Garlic Grunt Rub and place in the middle of the smoker. Smoke the turkey legs until they reach an internal temperature of 170°F (77°C).

ASIAN BBQ SHRIMP

Quick and easy appetizers are a must-have in your recipe library. This grilled Asian BBQ Shrimp recipe is simple, quick and quite impressive for your guests.

SERVES 2

1 cup (240 ml) ketchup

¼ cup (60 ml) yellow mustard

2 tbsp (30 ml) Asian fish sauce

¼ cup (60 ml) rice vinegar

¼ cup (60 g) light brown sugar

1 tsp gochujang

1 tsp grated fresh ginger

¼ tsp cayenne pepper

1 tsp soy sauce

½ tsp sesame oil

2 cloves garlic, grated

Salt

Freshly ground black pepper

1 lb (455 g) jumbo shrimp, peeled and deveined

Extra virgin olive oil

Toasted sesame seeds, for garnish

Chopped green onions, for garnish

In a medium saucepan, combine the ketchup, mustard, fish sauce, rice vinegar, brown sugar, gochujang, ginger, cayenne, soy sauce, sesame oil and garlic and a pinch each of salt and pepper. Bring the sauce to a boil, remove from the heat and allow the sauce to cool to room temperature. Set aside until ready to grill.

Soak some wooden skewers in water for a minimum of 20 minutes. This will slow down the charring and burning from the grill.

BIG GREEN EGG SETUP:

Fill your firebox with natural lump charcoal and prepare your Big Green Egg for direct grilling. The target grilling temperature is about 425°F (220°C) as indicated on your dome thermometer. Both the bottom vent and daisy wheel should be open about 50 percent, but small adjustments might be required. You want to create a mature fire with no flame. If you allow your Big Green Egg to burn at its target temperature, in this case 425°F (220°C), for at least 10 minutes, all the lit coals should be glowing orange without a flame—this is your indication that you have built a mature fire.

Thread the shrimp onto the skewers. Brush with olive oil and season with salt and pepper. Place the kebabs in the middle of the hot grill. Grill for 2 minutes on each side, then brush with the Asian barbecue sauce and grill for another minute per side to caramelize the sauce.

Sprinkle with toasted sesame seeds and green onions.

IN
BETWEEN
THE BUNS

Joseph Francis "Joey" Tribbiani Jr., Matt Leblanc's character from the TV show *Friends*, loved sandwiches. A couple of my friends and family call me Joey because of my passion for sandwiches. Here are some of my favorites.

MAPLE BRUNCH BURGERS
WITH FRIED EGG AND FRENCH-TOASTED BRIOCHE BUNS

This burger was one of my entries into the World Food Championship's Burger category. We loved the mix of sweet and savory in burger form.

MAKES 2 HEARTY BURGERS OR 4 (4-OZ [115-G]) BURGERS

BURGER

12 oz (340 g) ground chuck

4 oz (115 g) Jimmy Dean Maple Premium Pork Sausage

Kosher salt

Freshly ground black pepper

8 oz (225 g) bacon, cooked

Smoked Gouda cheese

BIG GREEN EGG SETUP:

Fill your firebox with natural lump charcoal and prepare your Big Green Egg for direct grilling. The target grilling temperature is 450°F (230°C) as indicated on your dome thermometer. You want to create a mature fire with no flame. If you allow your Big Green Egg to burn at its target temperature, in this case 450°F (230°C), for at least 10 minutes, all the lit coals should be glowing orange without a flame—this is your indication that you have built a mature fire.

PREPARE THE BURGER:

In a large bowl, mix the ground chuck and maple sausage together. Make sure to combine both proteins thoroughly but be careful not to overmix. A happy burger is a burger made with care! Separate the meat mixture into two 8-ounce (225-g) portions and form them into patties. If you're making four patties, divide the meat mixture into 4 equal patties. Remember to be gentle when forming your patties. Your end product should resemble a nicely formed hockey puck that is not too tightly packed.

Season the burgers liberally with salt and pepper on each side and place them in the refrigerator until you are ready to grill. At this stage, make sure your bacon is cooked. Don't forget the bacon! Please don't forget the bacon.

While you are waiting for your Big Green Egg to reach the desired cooking temperature by way of the mature fire described earlier, start mixing up the maple aioli and French toast batter.

(CONTINUED)

MAPLE AIOLI

½ cup (120 ml) mayonnaise

2 tbsp (9 g) pure maple sugar

1½ tbsp (8 g) light brown sugar

⅛ tsp freshly grated nutmeg

FRENCH TOAST

2 large eggs

1 tsp pure vanilla extract

2 tbsp (30 ml) pure maple syrup

¾ cup (175 ml) half-and-half

¼ tsp freshly grated nutmeg

2 tbsp (28 g) unsalted butter

2 or 4 brioche hamburger buns

TO ASSEMBLE

2 or 4 large eggs

Pinch of salt

Boston Bibb lettuce

PREPARE THE MAPLE AIOLI:

In a small bowl, combine all the aioli ingredients. Use a fork or whisk to mix thoroughly. Feel free to leave the finished product out on the counter while your burgers are cooking. Cold condiments on a burger will cool it down faster than those that are room temperature.

PREPARE THE FRENCH TOAST BATTER:

In a bowl, whisk the eggs, then add all the French toast ingredients, except the butter and buns, and mix thoroughly to incorporate. You have now created a maple custard that should be refrigerated until you are ready to cook the buns French toast–style.

THE COOK:

With the grill preheated, place a 12-inch (30-cm) cast-iron skillet directly on one side of the grill grate and preheat. The other side of the grill should be kept free and clear of the pan. This is where you will grill the burgers over the direct heat from the coals. Grill the patties for 4 to 5 minutes per side until they reach an internal temperature of 135 to 140°F (57 to 60°C), verified by an instant-read thermometer. Do not touch or move the patties after you place them on the grill. You should only touch the patties when you intend to flip them—moving a partially cooked burger is a recipe for having the burger stick to the grate.

Top the patties with the cheese once they are at about 120°F (49°C) internal temperature, about 6 minutes into the cook. This will ensure that the cheese is melted completely once the patties are done.

After the burgers are cooked, transfer to a clean plate and tent with foil. Let the burgers rest.

Add the butter to the heated cast-iron skillet. Dip the buns, cut side down, into the French toast batter and place them in the skillet to fry. Remove the buns once they are GBD. (That's grill talk for golden, brown and delicious!) Transfer from the skillet to a clean plate.

Use the now empty cast-iron skillet to fry your eggs. There should be enough butter left over in the skillet to fry the eggs. Crack each egg into the skillet, add a pinch of salt and fry until the whites are solid. If you do not like runny yolks, flip the eggs after the whites have become solid to make it over-easy or over-medium, based on your preference. However, you'll miss out on some incredible gooey yolk goodness.

ASSEMBLE THE BURGERS:

From the bottom to the top—slather the bottom bun with a generous amount of the maple aioli; add lettuce, the burger patty with melted cheese, bacon slices, an egg and the top bun (the crown, in chef-speak).

CHEF TIP: If you are really feeling "brunchy," dust the egg with powdered sugar before topping it with the bun. This takes the burger to a whole other level of decadence!

PASTRAMI'D TRI TIP SANDWICH

I am a huge fan of cured meats. I love the science behind the process and have been curing my own meats for several years. My favorite cured meat is pastrami. Although pastrami is typically made from beef brisket, you can "pastrami" cure any cut of beef. I like trying different and various cuts to see how each cut differs during the curing process. One of my favorite cuts to cure is tri tip, and I prefer it sliced thin on a sammie!

Note: This recipe requires 30 days for the giardiniera and 10 to 11 days' time for the tri tip.

SERVES 6

ITALIAN GIARDINIERA

1 celery rib, finely diced

1 carrot, finely diced

½ red bell pepper, seeded and diced

½ sweet onion, diced

¼ cup (73 g) salt

2 serrano peppers, sliced into ¼" (6-mm) slices or disks, with seeds

2 jalapeño peppers, sliced into ¼" (6-mm) slices or disks, with seeds

2 cloves garlic, minced

2 tsp (2 g) dried oregano

2 tsp (2 g) red pepper flakes

½ cup (120 ml) white vinegar

½ cup (120 ml) high-quality extra virgin olive oil

Pinch of freshly ground black pepper

¼ tsp cayenne pepper

PASTRAMI'D TRI TIP

1 gallon (3.8 L) water

1 cup (240 g) kosher salt

2 tsp (8 g) Prague powder #1 (pink curing salt)

8 dried bird's eye chiles

2 bay leaves

6 black peppercorns

Mishima Reserve Wagyu tri tip (generally 3½ lbs [1.6 kg])

Freshly ground black pepper

PREPARE THE ITALIAN GIARDINIERA:

In a 1-quart (1-L) Mason jar, combine all the giardiniera ingredients. Make sure that all the vegetables are covered with liquid. If not, add more olive oil until covered. Place the jar in a dark place for a minimum of 30 days before using. As you use the relish, make sure that the relish is covered with the oil.

PREPARE THE TRI TIP:

In a large bowl, combine the water, salt and Prague powder #1 and whisk. The mixture will turn cloudy immediately, but continue to whisk until the water turns clear. Clear water means that the salt and Prague powder #1 have dissolved. Add the chiles, bay leaves and peppercorns and mix well. Drop in the tri tip and allow to brine/cure for 10 days covered in the refrigerator.

(CONTINUED)

CARAMELIZED ONIONS

1 tbsp (15 ml) extra virgin olive oil

1 tbsp (14 g) unsalted butter

2 Vidalia onions, chopped

Salt and freshly ground black pepper

1 tbsp (13 g) sugar

Stone-ground mustard

1 baguette

BIG GREEN EGG SETUP:

Fill your firebox with natural lump charcoal and prepare your Big Green Egg for indirect smoking. Both the daisy wheel and bottom vent should be wide open during ignition. Use a torch or starter cubes to light the charcoal in a single spot to start a bed of coals. Allow the fire to burn for 10 minutes before making any damper adjustments. Add 4 or 5 chunks of smoking wood; I like hickory with steak. Both the bottom vent and daisy wheel should now be open about 10 percent. The target smoking temperature is about 250°F (120°C) as indicated on your dome thermometer. It is okay if you overshoot the target temperature. Just know that the hotter the fire, the less time will be needed to cook.

Remove the tri tip from the cure. It will look sort of gray from being submerged in the water for so long. Pat it dry with paper towels. Season the outside with black pepper only and place it in the center of the smoker. Allow to smoke until the tri tip reaches an internal temperature of 140°F (60°C). Remove from the smoker. Remove the ceramic diffuser from the smoker and open all the vents and daisy wheel to increase the temperature of the cooker to 600°F (315°C). Once that temperature is achieved, sear each side of the tri tip for 90 seconds. Remove from the grill and refrigerate overnight.

PREPARE THE CARAMELIZED ONIONS:

Heat a 12-inch (30-cm) skillet over medium-high heat on the stovetop. Add the oil and butter and allow the butter to melt. Add the onions, salt, pepper and sugar. Toss the onions to coat them with the liquid and seasoning. Sauté until the onions become soft and browned, 6 to 7 minutes.

TO ASSEMBLE YOUR SANDWICH:

Shave the cold pastrami. Spread the stone-ground mustard on a baguette. Add the smoked pastrami, then top with the caramelized onions and giardiniera.

COWBOY BURGER

There is nothing better than a great burger. I'm talking about a burger where the juices run past your hands and down to your elbows. For me, the perfect burger is savory, juicy and has some heat to it. Here's my perfect burger.

SERVES 4

BBQ SAUCE

1 cup (240 ml) ketchup

½ cup (115 g) light brown sugar

3 tbsp (45 ml) honey

1 tbsp (15 ml) yellow mustard

1 jalapeño pepper, seeded and minced

1 tbsp (15 ml) molasses

Pinch of paprika

¼ tsp cayenne pepper

1 tbsp (15 ml) Worcestershire sauce

½ tsp granulated garlic

½ tsp kosher salt

½ tsp coarsely ground black pepper

DEEP-FRIED JALAPEÑOS

½ cup (60 g) all-purpose flour

1 tsp salt

½ tsp cayenne pepper

1 tsp freshly ground black pepper

½ tsp paprika

1 large egg

½ cup (60 g) pickled jalapeño peppers, drained and dried on paper towels

Peanut oil, for frying

PREPARE THE BBQ SAUCE:

In a medium saucepan, combine all the sauce ingredients. Bring to a boil and then reduce the heat to low and simmer for 30 minutes. Refrigerate until ready to serve.

PREPARE THE DEEP-FRIED JALAPEÑOS:

In a small bowl, whisk together the flour, salt, cayenne, black pepper and paprika. In a separate bowl, beat the egg. Coat the jalapeños in the flour mixture, then in the egg wash, then back in the flour dredge. Meanwhile, in a deep-fryer or deep saucepan, heat the peanut oil to 350°F (180°C). Fry the breaded jalapeños for 3 to 4 minutes, or until golden brown.

BIG GREEN EGG SETUP:

Fill your firebox with natural lump charcoal and prepare your Big Green Egg for direct grilling. The target grilling temperature is about 450°F (230°C) as indicated on your dome thermometer. Both the bottom vent and daisy wheel should be open about 50 percent, but small adjustments might be required. You want to create a mature fire with no flame. If you allow your Big Green Egg to burn at its target temperature, in this case 450°F (230°C), for at least 10 minutes, all the lit coals should be glowing orange without a flame—this is your indication that you have built a mature fire.

(CONTINUED)

COWBOY BURGER (CONTINUED)

BURGERS

1 lb (455 g) Mishima Reserve Wagyu ground beef

8 oz (225 g) hot Italian sausage

Salt and freshly ground black pepper

TO ASSEMBLE

Toasted brioche buns

Shredded Cheddar Jack cheese

8 strips cooked bacon

PREPARE THE BURGERS:

In a medium bowl, mix together the ground beef and ground sausage. Form the mixture into four 8-ounce (225-g) patties, season with salt and pepper and place in the center of the hot grill. Grill the burgers for about 4 minutes per side to a medium internal temperature of 145°F (63°C).

ASSEMBLE THE BURGERS:

Smear the BBQ sauce on the cut sides of the bottom and top of each bun, add a burger patty, cheese, bacon and fried jalapeños, then top with the top bun.

TEQUILA LIME STEAK TACOS
WITH FIRE-ROASTED CORN SALSA

June 2018, I was having a grilling party at my house. We were doing tequila shots while cooking. I was mixing up a marinade for some skirt steak and a friend spilled a shot into my mixing bowl. I thought the marinade was ruined, but it turned out to be the best I've ever made! Sometimes accidents make things better!

SERVES 4

MARINADE

⅓ cup (80 ml) extra virgin olive oil

Zest and juice of 1 lime

1 oz (30 ml) premium tequila

¼ cup (10 g) chopped fresh cilantro

3 cloves garlic, smashed

1 jalapeño pepper, chopped, seeds included

1½ tsp (8 g) kosher salt

1 tsp freshly ground black pepper

½ tsp ground cumin

¼ tsp cayenne pepper

1 lb (455 g) skirt or flap steak

MARINATE THE STEAK:

In a gallon-sized (3.8-L) ziplock bag, combine all the marinade ingredients. As these bags are notorious for leaks when full of marinade, save yourself some cleanup time by placing the bag in a large bowl to catch any unwanted leaks. Seal the top and shake to mix together all the marinade components. Open the bag and add the whole, uncut steak to the mixture. Reseal the bag and shake to coat all areas of the steak. Open 1 corner of the bag, roll the bag on the counter, push out all the air out of the bag and then reseal. Place the steak-filled bag back in the large bowl and place into the refrigerator. Although this marinade can be done in 4 hours if you're in a pinch, a full 24-hour period will result in more flavor and a more tender bite. Turn the bag every time you open the refrigerator during the 24-hour marinating time. This will ensure even coverage.

BIG GREEN EGG SETUP:

Fill your firebox with natural lump charcoal and prepare your Big Green Egg for direct grilling. Light 3 starter cubes in a triangle to start a bed of coals. Both the bottom vent and daisy wheel will be open about 60 percent. The target grilling temperature is about 500°F (260°C) as indicated on your dome thermometer. All the lit coals should be glowing orange without a flame—this is your indication that you have built a mature fire. This will take about 10 minutes after your temperature is stabilized.

(CONTINUED)

CORN SALSA

Zest of 1 lime

Juice of 2 limes

2 vine-ripened tomatoes, diced

1 jalapeño pepper, seeded and minced

¼ onion, finely diced

1 cup (172 g) canned or cooked black beans, drained and rinsed

¼ cup (10 g) fresh cilantro, chopped

1½ tsp (8 g) kosher salt

½ tsp freshly ground black pepper

¼ cup (30 g) finely crumbled Cotija cheese

2 ears fresh corn, husks removed

PREPARE THE SALSA:

While you wait for the Big Green Egg to reach its desired cooking temperature, in a medium bowl, combine all the salsa ingredients except the corn. Give it a good stir and set aside to allow the flavors to meld together. Once the Big Green Egg is up to temperature, grill the corn. The corn will turn a bright yellow as it cooks, then will eventually begin to take on some char. Keep turning the corn until it is cooked evenly. You don't need to add any oil; just cook the corn as is until it's charred.

Remove the corn from the grill. Use a knife to cut off one of the ends off each ear, which will give you a flat and even end to help it stand up nicely. Then, cut the corn off the cob. Add the loose charred kernels to the salsa mixture and stir thoroughly.

THE COOK:

Remove the steak from the marinade. Remove any pieces of garlic or jalapeño that may stick to the steak.

Grill the marinated steak until it reaches an internal temperature of 140°F (60°C) as indicated on your instant-read thermometer. Grill on each side for about 6 minutes, remove from the heat and probe with a thermometer. If the steak is short of the target internal temperature, grill each side for an additional 30 seconds, remove and probe again. Repeat this step until the target temperature is achieved.

The steak should have a fair amount of caramelization on the outside. Rest the steak for about 7 minutes before slicing. Resting steak is important. During the resting period, the juices inside the meat will redistribute throughout the protein and result in a juicer end product.

TO ASSEMBLE

Corn tortillas

Cotija cheese, for serving (optional)

Fresh lime juice, for serving (optional)

While the steak rests, place a 12-inch (30-cm) cast-iron skillet on the grill grate and heat for 2 minutes. Place the tortillas, 1 at a time, in the dry skillet and cook for about 30 seconds per side. Wrap each in a clean dish towel after it is heated.

ASSEMBLE THE TACOS:

Slice the steak across the grain into pencil-width strips. Take your warm tortillas out of the dish towel, place several slices of steak in the middle and add a heaping spoonful of the fire-roasted corn salsa. Feel free to add more Cotija cheese and a squeeze of lime juice to finish.

CHEF TIPS: Have your dinner guests build their own tacos at the table! This will allow you to get food on the table quicker since you're saving time by not assembling each taco individually.

You probably will have leftover tequila—nothing goes better with tacos than tequila—so, feel free to enjoy while cooking or during dinner. Your Taco Tuesday just got even better!

NASHVEGAS HOT GRILLED CHICKEN SANDWICH

I like all things hot. I mean *hot*. Sometimes, it can't get hot or spicy enough. I went to Nashville several years ago and visited Hattie B's for the first time. I made a mistake and ordered the hottest sauce there, called Shut the Cluck Up. Well, it finally got hot enough for me. Ha! I loved it so much that it inspired me to create my own hot chicken sandwich.

SERVES 2

NASHVEGAS DRY RUB

1 tbsp (5 g) cayenne pepper

1 tbsp (15 g) packed light brown sugar

1 tbsp (18 g) salt

2 tsp (4 g) freshly ground black pepper

½ tsp paprika

½ tsp garlic powder

½ tsp onion powder

2 skinless, boneless chicken breasts

Extra virgin olive oil

PREPARE THE DRY RUB:

In a small bowl, combine all the rub ingredients and set aside.

BIG GREEN EGG SETUP:

Fill your firebox with natural lump charcoal and prepare your Big Green Egg for direct grilling. The target grilling temperature is about 450°F (230°C) as indicated on your dome thermometer. Both the bottom vent and daisy wheel should be open about 50 percent, but small adjustments might be required. You want to create a mature fire with no flame. If you allow your Big Green Egg to burn at its target temperature, in this case 450°F (230°C), for at least 10 minutes, all the lit coals should be glowing orange without a flame—this is your indication that you have built a mature fire.

Brush the chicken breasts with olive oil and then dust with the dry rub. Place in the center of the hot grill and grill the chicken to an internal temperature of 160°F (71°C). Remove from the grill and let rest for 6 to 8 minutes.

(CONTINUED)

CHICKEN DIP SAUCE

½ cup (104 g) lard

3 tbsp (16 g) cayenne pepper

1 tbsp (15 g) packed light brown sugar

1 tbsp (15 ml) honey

Salt and freshly ground black pepper

½ tsp paprika

½ tsp garlic powder

Arugula

Toasted brioche buns, split

Pickle slices, for serving

PREPARE THE SAUCE:

In a small saucepan, combine all the sauce ingredients. Bring to a boil and then lower the heat to a medium simmer. You need a medium simmer for serving.

Place a bed of arugula on the bottom of each toasted bun. Slice the chicken into sandwich-sized slices. Dunk each of the chicken slices into the hot sauce for 20 seconds. The sauce will semifry the chicken pieces and infuse the heat into them. Add the dunked chicken pieces to the sandwich and top with pickle slices.

PORK BELLY BAO
WITH ASIAN SLAW (HOW BAO DAT)

If you've never had a bao bun, you are really missing out. Bao are Chinese buns that are steamed to soft, fluffy pillows of perfection. I like to add some smoked pork belly and an Asian slaw for texture. So tasty!

SERVES 6

ASIAN SLAW

2 tbsp (30 ml) mayonnaise

2 tbsp (30 ml) Greek yogurt

4 tsp (20 ml) rice vinegar

2 tsp (10 ml) sesame oil

2 tsp (10 ml) soy sauce

2 tsp (15 g) gochujang

6 mini cucumbers, finely julienned

4 carrots, finely julienned

PORK

2 lbs (905 g) skin-off fresh pork belly

¼ cup (48 g) BBQ rub of your choice, something good with pork

PREPARE THE SLAW:

In a medium bowl, combine all the slaw ingredients and mix thoroughly. Refrigerate until ready to serve. The slaw is better after 3 to 4 hours in the refrigerator.

BIG GREEN EGG SETUP:

Fill your firebox with natural lump charcoal and prepare your Big Green Egg for indirect smoking. Both the daisy wheel and bottom vent should be wide open during ignition. Use a torch or starter cubes to light the charcoal in a single spot to start a bed of coals. Allow the fire to burn for 10 minutes before making any damper adjustments. Add 5 or 6 chunks of smoking wood layered between the charcoal; I like apple wood with pork. Both the bottom vent and daisy wheel should now be open about 5 percent. The target smoking temperature is about 225°F (110°C) as indicated on your dome thermometer. It is okay if you overshoot the target temperature. Just know that the hotter the fire, the less time will be needed to cook.

(CONTINUED)

PORK BELLY BAO (CONTINUED)

ASIAN BBQ SAUCE

1 cup (240 ml) sweet BBQ sauce

2 tbsp (30 ml) soy sauce

2 tbsp (30 ml) rice vinegar

1 tbsp (15 ml) fresh lemon juice

Zest of 1 lemon

1 tsp Asian fish sauce

1 tsp minced fresh ginger

½ tsp sesame oil

TO ASSEMBLE

12 fresh bao buns

PREPARE THE PORK:

Season the pork belly with the BBQ rub, ensuring that it's coated evenly, then place in the middle of the smoker. Smoke the belly until the internal temperature reaches 203°F (95°C) and it is probe tender all over.

PREPARE THE SAUCE:

In a small saucepan, combine all the sauce ingredients. Bring to a boil, then remove from the heat and allow to cool to room temperature.

Remove the pork belly from the cooker and allow it to rest for 20 minutes. Slice the belly into thin strips, dunk it into the BBQ sauce, then place inside the bao buns and top with the slaw.

FROM THE SEA

I've met so many people over the years in my grilling classes who are afraid of cooking seafood. Seafood is expensive and can easily be overcooked and ruined. There is a phrase in the barbecue/grilling world, "If you're lookin', you ain't cookin'." Although this is 100 percent true for a lot of things, it's the exact opposite for seafood. I spell the word seafood "seefood" on my grilling class notes to remind everyone to keep an eye on it when cooking. Every different piece of fish or crustacean will tell you visually when it is done. Here are my tips and tricks for cooking seafood to perfection.

SEARED SCALLOPS

A perfectly cooked scallop is like a present for your mouth. Crispy, crusty exterior with a tender interior is just pure perfection. If the scallops are cooked perfectly, there is no need to overcomplicate them with sauces or seasonings. Sometimes simplicity is winning!

SERVES 2

8 U8 scallops (U8 = 8 units per pound [455 g])

Salt and freshly ground black pepper

2 tbsp (30 ml) extra virgin olive oil

2 tbsp (28 g) unsalted butter

BIG GREEN EGG SETUP:

Fill your firebox with natural lump charcoal and prepare your Big Green Egg for direct grilling. Both the daisy wheel and bottom vent should be wide open during ignition. Use a torch or starter cubes to light the charcoal in a triangle shape to start a bed of coals. Allow the fire to burn for 10 minutes before making any damper adjustments. Both the bottom vent and daisy wheel should now be open about 70 percent. The target grilling temperature is about 400°F (200°C) as indicated on your dome thermometer. It is okay if you overshoot the target temperature. Just know that the hotter the fire, the less time will be needed to cook.

Place a 12-inch (30-cm) cast-iron skillet on the grill grate and allow it to heat for about 20 minutes.

Do not wash the scallops! They are already in their own liquid, so washing will remove some of that flavor. However, you will need to remove the foot from the scallop. The foot is the small tough piece of flesh that holds each scallop in its shell. Removing it is as simple as gently peeling it off and discarding it.

Season the scallops with salt and pepper. Leave the scallops in the refrigerator until ready to cook.

(CONTINUED)

SEARED SCALLOPS (CONTINUED)

Drizzle the olive oil into the skillet. Scallops have 2 sides: a larger, flat surface and a smaller, rounded surface. You'll want to place the flat surface in the skillet first. This will create a larger crust. The scallops will immediately stick to the pan. Relax; this is normal. The instant heat causes the scallops to tighten up. Sear for 1 minute, then add the butter. The butter will help with the caramelization on the crust of the scallop. Like most seafood, scallops will tell you when they are ready to be flipped, by releasing themselves from the skillet. I use a spatula to nudge them gently to see whether this has occurred. Once released, flip them over. You should have a beautiful golden-brown caramelized crust on your scallops. You will not get the same crust on the bottom of the scallops, so do not expect that. This is why we seared the larger surface first. Finish the scallops by cooking the smaller side for 2 minutes, basting with the butter and oil from the pan. Remove the scallops from the skillet and allow them to drain on a paper towel until ready to plate and serve.

JACK DANIEL'S TENNESSEE HONEY–GLAZED CEDAR-PLANKED SALMON

I like Jack Daniel's Tennessee Honey Whiskey two ways: frozen and poured over vanilla ice cream, and in a glaze on salmon. Here is my glaze and salmon recipe.

SERVES 4

1 cup (240 ml) + 6 tbsp (90 ml) Jack Daniel's Tennessee Honey Whiskey

1 cup (240 ml) + 6 tbsp (90 ml) water

2 cedar planks, each about 3" x 6" (7.5 x 15 cm)

1 tbsp (15 ml) extra virgin olive oil

5 cloves garlic, minced

6 tbsp (90 g) light brown sugar

2 tbsp (30 ml) fresh orange juice

2 tbsp (30 ml) low-sodium soy sauce

Zest of 1 orange

Salt and freshly ground black pepper

1 orange, peel on

1 red onion

4 skin-on salmon fillets

Toasted sesame seeds, for garnish

Chopped green onions, for garnish

Combine the cup (240 ml) of whiskey and cup (240 ml) of water in a large ziplock bag and soak the cedar planks overnight. No need to refrigerate.

BIG GREEN EGG SETUP:

Fill your firebox with natural lump charcoal and prepare your Big Green Egg for direct grilling. The target grilling temperature is about 425°F (220°C) as indicated on your dome thermometer. Both the bottom vent and daisy wheel should be open about 50 percent, but small adjustments might be required. You want to create a mature fire with no flame. If you allow your Big Green Egg to burn at its target temperature, in this case 425°F (220°C), for at least 10 minutes, all the lit coals should be glowing orange without a flame—this is your indication that you have built a mature fire.

Meanwhile, place a 12-inch (30-cm) skillet over medium-high heat on the stovetop. Add the extra virgin olive oil and sauté the garlic. Once the garlic has softened and is fragrant, add the remaining 6 tablespoons (90 ml) of whiskey and 6 tablespoons (90 ml) of water, brown sugar, orange juice and soy sauce. Zest the orange into the skillet and add a pinch each of salt and pepper. Bring this mixture to a boil, then immediately lower the heat to a slow simmer. Simmer for about 10 minutes, or until the mixture thickens into a glaze. Remove from the heat, but keep warm.

(CONTINUED)

JACK DANIEL'S TENNESSEE HONEY-GLAZED CEDAR-PLANKED SALMON (CONTINUED)

Remove the cedar planks from the plastic bag and pat dry with a paper towel. Slice the orange and onion in half and then into ¼-inch (6-mm) slices. Alternate the orange and onion slices to create a bed on top of each plank. This will create a bed for the salmon to sit on. Season the salmon with salt and pepper, then place 2 fillets skin side down on top of each orange and onion bed. Brush the fish with the glaze and place the planked fish directly onto the grill grate to start smoking and cooking.

The salmon will take 20 minutes to cook, depending on the thickness of the fish. This is one scenario where you will want to look and check often to ensure you are not overcooking the fish. You will want to brush the glaze over the salmon fillets several times throughout the cook. Cook the salmon until it has an internal temperature of 140 to 145°F (60 to 63°C). Salmon will tell you visually when it is done cooking and ready to eat. The fish will be flaky and the fat will start to turn white between the layers of flesh.

Once cooked through, remove from the heat. Garnish with toasted sesame seeds and green onions. Enjoy!

ROASTED WHOLE RED SNAPPER
WITH FRESH PISTOU SAUCE

Shopping for seafood can be tricky, especially when it comes to fish. Here are some signs that you are choosing fresh fish: First, fresh fish does not smell fishy. It should smell like the ocean. Second, the eyes should be clear. Old fish will have cloudy eyes, whereas the freshest fish will have clear eyes. Also, get to know your fishmonger. He or she will help you during the selection and in the processing of your fish. A good fishmonger will clean the fish for you, if you ask. I always get my snapper cleaned out and descaled and the fins removed.

SERVES 2

PISTOU SAUCE

1 clove garlic, chopped

Pinch of kosher salt

Pinch of freshly ground black pepper

1½ cups (36 g) fresh basil leaves, roughly chopped

1 small Roma tomato, peeled, seeded and chopped

¼ cup (60 ml) extra virgin olive oil

1 tsp lemon zest

1 tsp fresh lemon juice

¼ cup (25 g) grated Pecorino Romano cheese

PREPARE THE PISTOU SAUCE:

In a mortar, combine the garlic clove with a big pinch of kosher salt. The gritty salt will help smooth out the garlic. Use the pestle to grind the garlic into a smooth paste. Add the black pepper and basil along with the tomato and continue to crush and grind. Add the olive oil, lemon zest and juice and Pecorino Romano; continue to crush and grind until well combined. Refrigerate until ready to use.

BIG GREEN EGG SETUP:

Fill your firebox with natural lump charcoal and prepare your Big Green Egg for indirect smoking. Both the daisy wheel and bottom vent should be wide open during ignition. Use a torch or starter cubes to light the charcoal in a single spot to start a bed of coals. Allow the fire to burn for 10 minutes before making any damper adjustments. I do not add any smoking wood to fish. Both the bottom vent and daisy wheel should now be open about 40 percent. The target smoking temperature is about 400°F (200°C) as indicated on your dome thermometer. It is okay if you overshoot the target temperature. Just know that the hotter the fire, the less time will be needed to cook.

(CONTINUED)

ROASTED WHOLE RED SNAPPER (CONTINUED)

FISH

Whole red snapper (5 to 7 lbs [2.3 to 3.2 kg])

Extra virgin olive oil

2 cloves garlic, finely minced (use a Microplane)

Salt and freshly ground black pepper

1 lemon, thinly sliced

1 bunch tarragon

1 bunch dill

Nonstick spray, for grill (optional)

PREPARE THE RED SNAPPER:

Make 3 slices down to the bone on each side of the red snapper. This will allow the seasoning to penetrate deeper and also help the fish cook more evenly. Brush the fish with a thin layer of extra virgin olive oil. Open the cavity, rub the inside with the minced garlic and season with salt and pepper. Stuff the cavity with the lemon slices, tarragon and dill.

Brush oil or use a nonstick spray to lubricate a clean grill grate. Transfer the fish to the grill grate and roast for about 20 minutes. The target internal temperature is between 133 and 137°F (56 and 58°C).

Remove the fish from the grill and transfer to a serving plate or platter. Spoon the pistou sauce over the fish.

CIOPPINO

Whether it's a cold rainy day or a summer day at the beach, cioppino can be a great dish to enjoy! Originating in San Francisco, this regional Italian-American dish satisfies your craving for seafood.

SERVES 4

Extra virgin olive oil

½ yellow onion, diced

5 cloves garlic, minced

8 oz (225 g) calamari, rings and tentacles

1 cup (240 ml) white wine

1 (15-oz [425-g]) can crushed tomatoes, with liquid

2 cups (475 ml) chicken stock, plus more if needed

Salt and freshly ground black pepper

½ tsp dried basil

Red pepper flakes

8 oz (225 g) littleneck clams, scrubbed

8 oz (225 g) white fish (something firm, such as monkfish), cubed

8 oz (225 g) scallops, feet removed

½ cup (30 g) chopped fresh parsley, divided

8 oz (225 g) shrimp, peeled and deveined

8 oz (225 g) mussels, scrubbed and debearded

1 baguette

BIG GREEN EGG SETUP:

Fill your firebox with natural lump charcoal and prepare your Big Green Egg for direct grilling. The target grilling temperature is about 400°F (200°C) as indicated on your dome thermometer. You want to create a mature fire with no flame. If you allow your Big Green Egg to burn at its target temperature, in this case 400°F (200°C), for at least 10 minutes, all the lit coals should be glowing orange without a flame—this is an indication that you have built a mature fire.

Heat a 6-quart (5.7-L) Dutch oven on the grill for about 10 minutes. Meanwhile, gather your mise en place. *Mise en place* is a French term for "everything in its place." In other words, all of your prep and knife work needs to be done prior to starting this dish. After you've prepped the seafood, stick it back in the refrigerator to keep it cold.

Once the Dutch oven is hot, drizzle in about 3 tablespoons (45 ml) of extra virgin olive oil. Add the onion and sauté. Keep the onion moving as you don't want it to brown, but just turn translucent and soften. Once the onion has softened, add the garlic and the calamari.

(CONTINUED)

CIOPINNO (CONTINUED)

All the seafood cooks for different times, so it is important to follow these steps. Sauté the calamari for 3 minutes, then add the white wine. Allow the wine to deglaze the pan and simmer for 3 minutes. Now, add the crushed tomatoes and chicken stock and stir thoroughly. Season with salt and black pepper, basil and red pepper flakes to taste, cover and bring to a simmer. You'll know if you need more liquid by the way the liquid looks. If it's reducing too much to the point where the ingredients aren't covered with the liquid, add more stock or water to increase the level of liquid above the other ingredients.

Simmer for 10 minutes before adding the clams and white fish. Simmer for 3 minutes and check whether the clams are opening up. When they are starting to open, add the scallops and half of the parsley. Simmer for 3 minutes. Add the shrimp and mussels, simmer for 1 minute, then remove the Dutch oven from the grill. Leave covered for 5 minutes. Garnish with the remaining parsley to serve.

Slice the baguette in half, brush with extra virgin olive oil and toast on the grill. Serve alongside the cioppino to soak up all of that delicious broth!

SEAFOOD PAELLA

My family and I spent some time in Barcelona in 2013. Of course, we wanted to experience authentic paella. I spent about 160 euros (about $190 US back then) on a seafood paella for four. It was terrible. Ha! I spent the entire flight home thinking about how I could make one better. Here is the recipe.

SERVES 4 OR 5

Large pinch of saffron threads

2 to 3 tbsp (30 to 45 ml) hot water

4 cups (946 ml) chicken stock

1 lb (455 g) large shrimp, peeled and deveined

Kosher salt and freshly ground black pepper

1 tsp paprika, divided

1 lb (455 g) mussels, clams or a combination

1 lb (455 g) littleneck clams

2 lobster tails, halved (optional)

8 oz (225 g) chorizo or andouille sausage, cut into ¼" (6-mm)-thick rounds

BIG GREEN EGG SETUP:

Fill your firebox with natural lump charcoal and prepare your Big Green Egg for direct grilling. The target grilling temperature is about 450°F (230°C) as indicated on your dome thermometer. Both the bottom vent and daisy wheel should be open about 50 percent, but small adjustments might be required. You want to create a mature fire with no flame. If you allow your Big Green Egg to burn at its target temperature, in this case 450°F (230°C), for at least 10 minutes, all the lit coals should be glowing orange without a flame—this is an indication that you have built a mature fire.

Allow the paella pan to heat on your Egg. Starting with a hot pan is essential.

While the pan heats, in a small bowl or cup, combine the saffron and the hot water. Stir thoroughly. This will release the flavor and all the yellow coloring.

In a medium saucepan on your stovetop, heat the chicken stock over low heat.

Season the shrimp with salt, pepper and ½ teaspoon of paprika, then refrigerate until needed.

Scrub and rinse the mussels, clams and lobster tails (if using).

Now that the paella pan is hot, add the sausage. As the sausage cooks, it will provide flavored oil for the rest of the ingredients. Cook until browned on both sides, about 5 minutes. It is not necessary to cook this all the way through. It will be added to the whole mixture later. Once cooked, remove from the pan and set aside in a bowl.

(CONTINUED)

1 lb (455 g) boneless, skinless chicken thighs, cut into 1" (2.5-cm) pieces

1 to 2 tbsp (15 to 30 ml) extra virgin olive oil

1 onion, diced small

4 cloves garlic, finely chopped

2 ripe tomatoes, diced

1 (6-oz [170-g]) bag frozen peas

2 cups (400 g) uncooked paella rice, labeled Valencia; Arborio can be substituted

2 tbsp (8 g) coarsely chopped fresh flat-leaf parsley leaves, for garnish

2 lemons, quartered, for serving

Now, add the chicken to the paella pan, spreading it evenly in the pan. Season with salt, pepper and ¼ teaspoon of paprika. Remember to season it again after it has been flipped. Cook until browned on all sides, about 5 minutes. Again, it is not critical that the pieces are cooked thoroughly. Once cooked, remove from the heat and add to the same bowl as the sausage.

At this point, add some extra virgin olive oil, if needed. Add the onion and garlic and sauté until translucent. Then, add the tomatoes, peas, rice and saffron mixture. Mix thoroughly to combine. The rice will start to take on the yellow color of the saffron.

Mix in the sausage and chicken. Once combined, spread the mixture evenly over the entire pan. How the mixture is placed will affect the final presentation. Once spread, add your warm chicken stock. Simmer for 10 to 13 minutes.

Add the seafood. I like to push my shellfish down into the rice mixture. They will release flavor into the broth that is left. Add the shrimp evenly across the top. Cook until the shellfish have opened and the rice is al dente. Remove from the heat. Allow the paella to rest for 5 to 7 minutes before serving. Garnish with the parsley and serve with quartered lemons.

NOTE: Clams need a longer cook time than mussels and shrimp. Consider adding them several minutes before the other seafood.

Saute the andouille.

Add the broth to the rest of the ingredients.

Let the broth cook down.

FIRE-ROASTED CHIPOTLE LIME OYSTERS

Quick and easy appetizers are essential to any dinner party. I always have several oyster knives on hand and I put my dinner guests to work! I'll show them how to shuck a couple oysters, then the rest is up to them. Here's how I cook them.

SERVES 2

1 dozen oysters

½ cup (112 g/1 stick) unsalted butter, at room temperature

Zest of 1 lime

Juice of 1 lime

1 large clove garlic, finely grated (use a Microplane)

1 chipotle chile, minced

2 tbsp (30 ml) adobo sauce

Pinch of salt

Pinch of freshly ground black pepper

BIG GREEN EGG SETUP:

Fill your firebox with natural lump charcoal and prepare your Big Green Egg for direct grilling. The target grilling temperature is about 550°F (290°C) as indicated on your dome thermometer. Both the bottom vent and daisy wheel should be open about 60 percent, but small adjustments might be required. You want to create a mature fire with no flame. If you allow your Big Green Egg to burn at its target temperature, in this case 550°F (290°C), for at least 10 minutes, all the lit coals should be glowing orange without a flame—this is an indication that you have built a mature fire.

Scrub all the oysters under cold running water. Remove any dirt or debris from the shells. Refrigerate, uncovered, until ready to grill.

In a medium bowl, combine the rest of the ingredients and mix with a fork.

Use an oyster knife to shuck the oysters: Hold an oyster with 1 hand, then use the other hand to place the tip of the knife into the hinge of the oyster. Add some pressure with the knife and twist. The knife will break the hinge and allow the oyster to open. Each oyster has a flat shell and a curved shell. Place the shucked oyster in the curved shell so that all the liquid remains inside the shell.

Place a spoonful of the butter mixture onto each of the oysters. Place the oyster, in its half-shell, in the center of the hot grill. Keep an eye on the oysters because each oyster is a different size with a different thickness shell and will cook at a different time. Once the oysters start bubbling in their shells, remove them from the grill. The shells will help keep them hot while you wait on the rest to finish.

SESAME-CRUSTED AHI TUNA STEAK
WITH SRIRACHA MAYO

My wife and I love tuna steaks. Whether on a salad or plated with rice, it is one of our favorite fish dishes. This ain't no chicken of the sea!

SERVES 2

¼ cup (60 ml) Duke's mayonnaise

¾ tsp sriracha

1 tsp soy sauce

2 tbsp (16 g) white sesame seeds

2 tbsp (16 g) black sesame seeds

2 thick-cut ahi tuna steaks (typically 4 to 6 oz [115 to 170 g])

Grapeseed oil

Salt and freshly ground black pepper

Pinch of cayenne pepper

In a small bowl, whisk together the mayonnaise, sriracha and soy sauce. Refrigerate until ready to serve.

BIG GREEN EGG SETUP:

Fill your firebox with natural lump charcoal and prepare your Big Green Egg for direct grilling. Both the daisy wheel and bottom vent should be wide open during ignition. Use a torch or starter cubes to light the charcoal in a triangle shape to start a bed of coals. Allow the fire to burn for 10 minutes before making any damper adjustments. Both the bottom vent and daisy wheel should now be open about 60 percent. The target grilling temperature is about 400°F (200°C) as indicated on your dome thermometer. It is okay if you overshoot the target temperature. Just know that the hotter the fire, the less time will be needed to cook.

Place a 12-inch (30-cm) cast-iron skillet on the grill grate and allow to heat for about 20 minutes. In a separate small bowl, combine the white and black sesame seeds and mix together to evenly disperse the colors. Brush the tuna steaks with grapeseed oil, season with salt, black pepper and cayenne and dip each side into the sesame seed mixture. The seeds should stick to the tuna steaks, creating a crust. Refrigerate the steaks until ready to cook.

Once the skillet is hot, drizzle in some of the grapeseed oil. Grapeseed oil has a higher smoking temperature than other commonly used oils, such as extra virgin olive oil and canola. Place the steaks in the skillet. Leave the dome open! Like most seafood, the tuna steaks will tell you visually when they are done: as they cook, you will see them turn from the pink raw flesh to an opaque white. I prefer to cook my tuna steaks rare with a hard seared crust. As you see the white opaque fish cooking up the side of the fish, flip when your desired doneness can be seen. Cook the other side to match. There is no real time frame because this is a visual cook. Drizzle the sriracha mayo over the fish.

COLOSSAL LOBSTER TAIL

When it comes to seafood, less is more. I like to let the seafood shine on its own vs. having a ton of complex sauces. Grilled lobster and a simple clarified butter hits the right spot.

SERVES 2

1 cup (225 g/2 sticks) unsalted butter

1 (28-oz [800-g]) lobster tail

Extra virgin olive oil

Salt and freshly ground black pepper

BIG GREEN EGG SETUP:

Fill your firebox with natural lump charcoal and prepare your Big Green Egg for direct grilling. The target grilling temperature is about 450°F (220°C) as indicated on your dome thermometer. Both the bottom vent and daisy wheel should be open about 50 percent, but small adjustments might be required. You want to create a mature fire with no flame. If you allow your Big Green Egg to burn at its target temperature, in this case 450°F (220°C), for at least 10 minutes, all the lit coals should be glowing orange without a flame—this is an indication that you have built a mature fire.

CLARIFY THE BUTTER:

Butter has 3 components: (1) milkfat, (2) butterfat and (3) water. Time to separate them. In a small saucepan, melt the butter over low heat, but do not bring to a boil. The butter will start to separate in the pan. Skim off the white milkfat from the top. Then, ladle off the middle layer of butterfat and reserve. Discard the bottom water layer. Keep the clarified butterfat warm until ready to serve.

This tail is huge, so it is necessary to cut the top of the shell with kitchen shears before slicing in half with your knife. Drive the knife all the way through to the bottom of your cutting board to create 2 lobster halves. Brush the flesh of the tail with extra virgin olive oil and then season with salt and pepper.

Place the flesh side of the tail on the hot grill and grill for 1 minute. Flip the tail and finish grilling it flesh side up. The shell will change from dark to bright red. Brush the flesh with clarified butter. (Be careful; the butter will create flare-ups if it hits the lit coals.) Grill the lobster to an internal temperature of 140°F (60°C). Serve it hot with a side of clarified butter for dipping.

ON THE SIDE

Good barbecue can stand alone, although some tasty sides can help the overall experience. Here are some of my favorites.

SMOKED MAC & CHEESE

While the smoke is rolling with your barbecue proteins, you might as well throw on some mac & cheese! You could almost call this cheese & mac. This ain't no Velveeta mac!

SERVES 8 TO 10

1 lb (455 g) uncooked elbow macaroni

1 (1-lb [455-g]) block pepper Jack cheese

1 (1-lb [455-g]) block mild Cheddar cheese

1 (1-lb [455-g]) block mozzarella cheese

1 cup (240 ml) whole milk

½ cup (120 ml) heavy cream

1 large egg

2 large egg yolks

½ cup (112 g/1 stick) unsalted butter, melted

2 tsp (10 g) kosher salt

1 tsp black pepper

2 tsp (4 g) cayenne pepper

½ tsp dry mustard

½ tsp freshly grated nutmeg

2 tbsp (14 g) smoked paprika

BIG GREEN EGG SETUP:

Fill your firebox with natural lump charcoal and prepare your Big Green Egg for indirect smoking. Both the daisy wheel and bottom vent should be wide open during ignition. Use a torch or starter cubes to light the charcoal in a single spot to start a bed of coals. Allow the fire to burn for 10 minutes before making any damper adjustments. Add 5 or 6 chunks of smoking wood layered between the charcoal; I typically use whatever wood is already smoking for my protein. Both the bottom vent and daisy wheel should now be open about 40 percent. The target smoking temperature is about 400°F (200°C) as indicated on your dome thermometer. It is okay if you overshoot the target temperature. Just know that the hotter the fire, the less time will be needed to cook.

In a large saucepan, boil the macaroni until al dente. *Al dente* means "firm to the bite." If a package calls for 10 minutes of boil, I usually go for 8 minutes. Drain and allow to cool to room temperature so it doesn't melt the cheese during assembly. Shred the pepper Jack, Cheddar and mozzarella cheese into separate bowls. I use block cheese because packaged shredded cheese has an anticlumping additive to keep it separated in the package. Block cheese does not have this additive, which results in a much more melty cheesy goodness. Shredding the cheese only takes a couple of minutes with a box grater.

You'll need a pretty large bowl for this next part. Mix together the milk, heavy cream, egg, yolks and melted butter with a whisk. Once smooth, add the salt, black pepper, cayenne, mustard and nutmeg. Dump in the cooled pasta and stir to make sure it is all coated with the milk mixture. Add three-quarters of each kind of shredded cheese and stir until completely incorporated. Dump into a foil half pan. Cover the top evenly with the remaining one-quarter of each shredded cheese. Dust the smoked paprika over the cheese. Place in the center of the smoker and smoke, uncovered, at 250°F (120°C) for about 1 hour, or until the top starts to brown. Remove from the smoker and allow the mac and cheese to cool for about 20 minutes before serving. This will allow the mac and cheese to set and firm up.

MEXICAN STREET CORN
(ELOTE)

Street food is at its peak in popularity all over the world. Walking the streets sure would be better with some mobile food! Folding the husk back on an ear of corn acts like a built-in handle!

SERVES 4

½ cup (120 ml) Duke's mayonnaise

1 tbsp (6 g) lime zest

1 tbsp (15 ml) lime juice

1 tbsp (15 ml) adobo sauce

Salt and freshly ground black pepper

1 tsp chili powder

4 ears of yellow corn, in their husks

½ cup (60 g) grated Cotija cheese

½ cup (20 g) finely chopped fresh cilantro

Lime slice, for garnish

In a small bowl, combine the mayonnaise, lime zest and juice, adobo sauce, salt, pepper and chili powder and mix thoroughly. Refrigerate until ready to serve.

BIG GREEN EGG SETUP:

Fill your firebox with natural lump charcoal and prepare your Big Green Egg for direct grilling. The target grilling temperature is about 400°F (200°C) as indicated on your dome thermometer. You want to create a mature fire with no flame. If you allow your Big Green Egg to burn at its target temperature, in this case 400°F (200°C), for at least 10 minutes, all the lit coals should be glowing orange without a flame—this is an indication that you have built a mature fire. Both the bottom vent and daisy wheel will be open about 30 percent.

Place the ears of corn, in their husks, on the grill grate. Grill for 15 minutes, turning constantly until most of each husk is charred. Remove from the grill. Peel back the husks and keep for easy handling, or peel off the charred husks and discard. Place the peeled ears of corn back onto the grill. Grill, turning constantly, until the corn starts to char on the exterior on all sides. Remove from the grill.

Stand up each ear of corn in a medium bowl and slice the corn kernels off the cob. Mix the sauce into the corn kernels. Sprinkle with the Cotija cheese and cilantro. Garnish with a slice of lime.

SMOKED APPLE BAKED BEANS

I like beans! I like apple pie! Oops, I merged them together! This baked beans recipe tastes like Grandma's apple pie!

SERVES 8 TO 10

1 lb (455 g) dried navy beans

2 Granny Smith apples, peeled, cored and chopped in ¼" (6-mm) pieces

½ Vidalia onion, diced

¼ cup (60 ml) Worcestershire sauce

¼ cup (60 ml) prepared yellow mustard

½ cup (120 ml) ketchup

¼ cup (60 ml) honey

4 strips bacon, browned and chopped

3 tbsp (45 ml) hot sauce (I use Frank's Red Hot)

2 tbsp (36 g) salt

1 tbsp (6 g) freshly ground black pepper

3 tbsp (45 ml) molasses

1½ cups (338 g) light brown sugar

2 tsp (4 g) cayenne pepper

Rinse the beans with cold water. In a medium saucepan, cover the beans with 2 inches (5 cm) of water and allow them to soak overnight. Drain the beans. Cover the beans with the same amount of cold water and bring to a boil. Lower the heat to low and let the beans simmer, covered, for 90 minutes, until the beans are tender. Drain the beans and allow to cool.

BIG GREEN EGG SETUP:

Fill your firebox with natural lump charcoal and prepare your Big Green Egg for indirect smoking. Both the daisy wheel and bottom vent should be wide open during ignition. Use a torch or starter cubes to light the charcoal in a single spot to start a bed of coals. Allow the fire to burn for 10 minutes before making any damper adjustments. Both the bottom vent and daisy wheel should now be open about 40 percent. The target smoking temperature is about 400°F (200°C) as indicated on your dome thermometer. It is okay if you overshoot the target temperature. Just know that the hotter the fire, the less time will be needed to cook.

In a large bowl, combine all the ingredients and fold, using a wooden spoon or spatula, until thoroughly and evenly mixed. Dump the mixture into a 12-inch (30-cm) seasoned cast-iron skillet. Place the skillet in the center of a 400°F (200°C) grill grate and roast for about 1 hour, or until the liquid is bubbling and the beans are tender and sweet.

TWICE-SMOKED TATERS

My kids love these twice-smoked taters and beg for them on the regular. They love the ultrarich and creamy potato filling. Don't worry; adults love them, too!

SERVES 4

4 russet potatoes, washed and dried

Extra virgin olive oil

Kosher salt

3 tbsp (42 g) cold unsalted butter

½ cup (115 g) sour cream

3 large egg yolks

Salt and freshly ground black pepper

1 tbsp (7 g) paprika

1 tsp cayenne pepper

8 strips bacon, cooked until crisp and crumbled, divided

¼ cup (12 g) diced fresh chives, divided

2 cups (240 g) shredded Gouda cheese, divided

¼ cup (55 g/½ stick) unsalted butter, melted

BIG GREEN EGG SETUP:

Fill your firebox with natural lump charcoal and prepare your Big Green Egg for indirect roasting. Both the daisy wheel and bottom vent should be wide open during ignition. Use a torch or starter cubes to light the charcoal in a single spot to start a bed of coals. Allow the fire to burn for 10 minutes before making any damper adjustments. I do not add any smoking wood. Both the bottom vent and daisy wheel should now be open about 30 percent. The target smoking temperature is about 400°F (200°C) as indicated on your dome thermometer. It is okay if you overshoot the target temperature. Just know that the hotter the fire, the less time will be needed to cook.

Brush the potatoes with extra virgin olive oil and sprinkle with a liberal amount of salt, then place them directly on the grill grate. Roast the potatoes for 1 hour, or until you can stick a paring knife into the top and the potato will fall off under its own weight. Remove the potatoes from the grill and allow them to cool until they can be handled. Once cool enough to handle, slice off the top quarter of each potato. Spoon out all the soft flesh of the potatoes into a medium bowl. Drop in the cold butter and mash the potatoes. The cold butter will help cool down the fluffy potatoes. Once completely mashed, form a well in the center of the potatoes. Add the sour cream and egg yolks. Start by mixing the sour cream and egg yolks together, then slowly start mixing in the surrounding potato. Do not omit the cold butter and sour cream, because adding the egg yolks to the hot potato will cause them to scramble. Season the mixture with salt and black pepper and the paprika and cayenne. Stir in three-quarters of the bacon, half of the chives and 1½ cups (180 g) of the cheese.

Spoon the filling into the skinned potato shells. Overfill the shells past the top. Use the back of a spoon to smooth out and round the top of each potato's filling. Use the prongs of a fork to create divots all over the top of the filling. Brush the tops with the melted butter. The butter should well into all the divots. Finally, garnish the tops with the remaining cheese, bacon and chives. Place the potatoes back on the grill, filling side up, for about 20 minutes, or until golden brown on top.

FRIED GREEN TOMATOES
WITH CHIPOTLE RÉMOULADE

My mother likes to grow tomatoes, but the squirrels like to eat them. We started pulling them while they were still green just so the little varmints wouldn't get them! But what do you do with a ton of green tomatoes? You fry them, that's what you do.

SERVES 4

1 (7-oz [198-g]) can chipotle chiles in adobo, minced

Zest and juice of ½ lime

¾ cup (175 ml) Duke's mayonnaise

¼ cup (10 g) fresh cilantro, finely chopped

Salt and freshly ground black pepper

1 tbsp (7 g) paprika

1 tsp dried basil

1 qt (946 ml) peanut oil

3 large green tomatoes

1 cup (125 g) all-purpose flour

3 large eggs

1 cup (60 g) panko bread crumbs

In a medium bowl, combine the chipotle chiles, lime zest and juice, mayonnaise, cilantro, salt, pepper, paprika and basil and mix into a rémoulade. Refrigerate until time to serve.

BIG GREEN EGG SETUP:

Fill your firebox with natural lump charcoal and prepare your Big Green Egg for direct grilling. The target grilling temperature is about 400°F (200°C) as indicated on your dome thermometer. You want to create a mature fire with no flame. If you allow your Big Green Egg to burn at its target temperature, in this case 400°F (200°C), for at least 10 minutes, all the lit coals should be glowing orange without a flame—this is an indication that you have built a mature fire.

Fill a cast-iron Dutch oven with the oil. This is potentially dangerous, so it is important to have a skillet or Dutch oven with high sides while frying over a live fire, to avoid any splattering of oil into the coals. Allow the oil to come up to 350°F (180°C).

Slice the tomatoes into ¼-inch (6-mm)-thick slices. Line up 3 shallow bowls. In one, place the flour. In the second, beat the eggs thoroughly to create an egg wash. In the third, place the bread crumbs. Dip the raw tomato slices into the flour, then into the egg wash, then into the bread crumbs. Be sure they are covered completely. Place the breaded tomato slices, 3 or 4 at a time, into the hot oil. Do not overcrowd the Dutch oven or it will cool down the oil. The tomatoes will need to be flipped to be cooked evenly. Fry the tomatoes until cooked to a golden brown. Drain on a paper towel–lined plate and serve with the chipotle rémoulade.

BOURBON CANDIED CARROTS

My mother always made sure we ate our vegetables. She'd say, "Carrots will make your eyes see better." Well, I've worn glasses for 20 years. Ha! I figure if I have to eat them, they should be candied with bourbon!

SERVES 2 OR 3

2 lbs (905 g) young carrots with stems and tops

½ cup (112 g/1 stick) unsalted butter

Kosher salt

Freshly ground black pepper

1 cup (225 g) light brown sugar

½ cup (120 ml) bourbon

1 tsp ground cinnamon

1 tsp freshly grated nutmeg

½ tsp ground cloves

2 tbsp (30 ml) honey

Pinch of cayenne pepper

BIG GREEN EGG SETUP:

Fill your firebox with natural lump charcoal and prepare your Big Green Egg for direct grilling. The target grilling temperature is about 300°F (150°C) as indicated on your dome thermometer. You want to create a mature fire with no flame. If you allow your Big Green Egg to burn at its target temperature, in this case 300°F (150°C), for at least 10 minutes, all the lit coals should be glowing orange without a flame—this is an indication that you have built a mature fire. Both the bottom vent and daisy wheel will be open about 20 percent.

Start by heating a 12-inch (30-cm) cast-iron skillet on the grill over the direct heat.

Chop off most of the green tops from the carrots but leave about ¾ inch (2 cm). Scrub and rinse the carrots under cold running water. Place them on a paper towel and allow to dry. Once dry, use a vegetable peeler to peel the raw outer skin off each carrot.

Drop the butter into the hot cast-iron skillet. Allow the butter to melt completely before adding the carrots. Stir the carrots to completely cover with the butter and allow them to cook for 10 minutes, stirring constantly to prevent overbrowning or burning.

The carrots should be halfway tender after the 10 minutes of cooking. Add the remaining ingredients to the skillet and stir to combine and coat the carrots. Cook for another 10 minutes, stirring constantly. (Have you gotten the stirring theme yet?!) The sugar will melt, the alcohol in the bourbon will burn off and the carrots will be candied.

HOT SMOKED TATER SALAD

Similar to a German potato salad, this hot smoked tater salad is perfect for any get-together.

SERVES 3 OR 4

2½ lbs (1.1 kg) red potatoes

½ cup (115 g) sour cream

3 tbsp (45 ml) white vinegar

1 tbsp (15 ml) hot sauce

½ cup (40 g) crispy, chopped bacon

1 tbsp (15 g) kosher salt

1½ tsp (3 g) freshly ground black pepper

¼ tsp cayenne pepper

¼ tsp red pepper flakes

¼ cup (25 g) chopped green onion (chopped on the bias)

½ tsp garlic powder

½ tsp celery salt

BIG GREEN EGG SETUP:

Fill your firebox with natural lump charcoal and prepare your Big Green Egg for indirect smoking. Both the daisy wheel and bottom vent should be wide open during ignition. Use a torch or starter cubes to light the charcoal in a single spot to start a bed of coals. Allow the fire to burn for 10 minutes before making any damper adjustments. Add 5 or 6 chunks of smoking wood layered between the charcoal; I typically use whatever wood is already smoking from my protein. Both the bottom vent and daisy wheel should now be open about 10 percent. The target smoking temperature is about 250°F (120°C) as indicated on your dome thermometer. It is okay if you overshoot the target temperature. Just know that the hotter the fire, the less time will be needed to cook.

While the Egg heats, bring a large pot of water to a boil on the stovetop and prepare an ice bath (a bowl filled partway with 50/50 ice and water). Meanwhile, scrub and rinse the potatoes under cold running water. Chop them into equal-sized eighths. Drop the potatoes into the boiling water and boil for exactly 7 minutes. Remove them immediately and drop them into the ice bath to cool. Once cool, drain the potatoes in a colander and allow them to air dry.

In a large bowl, whisk together all the other ingredients. Use a spatula to fold in the cooled potatoes and coat them thoroughly. Dump the mixture into a 12-inch (30-cm) cast-iron skillet or other heatproof vessel, place on the grill and smoke the potato salad for 12 to 15 minutes, or until the potatoes have taken on smoke and turned a golden color.

FULLY BAKED

So far, I've covered grilling, smoking and roasting. Now, let's bake. Yes, your Kamado will do that, too!

NEAPOLITAN-STYLE PIZZA

There is a lot of controversy over whether to cook pizza sauce. Some say it cooks on the pizza. Others say it needs to be cooked so that all the flavors meld together. My wife's Grandma Marie was from Naples, Italy. Grandma Marie cooked her pizza sauce, so we cook ours. Don't be scared by the dough measurements—you need to weigh the ingredients to get this right.

MAKES FOUR 14" (35-CM) PIZZAS

GRANDMA MARIE'S PIZZA SAUCE

1 tbsp (15 ml) extra virgin olive oil

¼ onion, diced

2 cloves garlic, minced

Crushed red pepper flakes (optional)

Salt and freshly ground black pepper

1 (28-oz [800-g]) can crushed tomatoes, with liquid

1 tbsp (3 g) dried oregano

DOUGH

790 g 00 pizza flour, plus more for dusting

474 g room-temperature water

16 g kosher salt

2.34 g active dry yeast

1 tsp extra virgin olive oil

PREPARE THE SAUCE:

In a 6-quart (5.7-L) pot over medium-high heat, combine the extra virgin olive oil, onion, garlic, red pepper flakes (if using) and salt and black pepper to taste. Constantly stirring and moving the ingredients, sauté until the onion is translucent. Then, add the crushed tomatoes and oregano. Cover and bring to a light boil, then lower the heat to a low simmer and cook for about 30 minutes, stirring occasionally. Season with additional salt and pepper to taste. Remove from the heat and allow to cool before adding to the pizza. Refrigerate until ready to use.

PREPARE THE DOUGH:

In a stand mixer fitted with the dough hook, combine all the dough ingredients, except the olive oil. Mix for 10 minutes on low speed. The dough should form a ball with the sides of the bowl clean. Coat a separate bowl with the olive oil. Drop in the dough ball and roll it to coat completely with the oil. The oil will prevent the dough from forming a crust during fermentation. Cover with plastic wrap and place in the refrigerator for 24 hours.

Four hours before you are ready to cook the pizzas, remove the dough from the bowl and cut into 4 equal-sized pieces. Form each piece into a ball by pulling and tucking the edges. Place the dough balls on a floured cookie sheet, dust the tops with flour, then cover with a clean dish towel and allow the dough balls to rise for 4 hours.

(CONTINUED)

NEAPOLITAN-STYLE PIZZA (CONTINUED)

TO ASSEMBLE

Semolina flour, for sprinkling

6 oz (170 g) mozzarella cheese, for sprinkling

6 fresh basil leaves

Extra virgin olive oil

BIG GREEN EGG SETUP:

Fill your firebox with natural lump charcoal and prepare your Big Green Egg for indirect roasting. Both the daisy wheel and bottom vent should be wide open during ignition. Use a torch or starter cubes to light the charcoal in a single spot to start a bed of coals. Allow the fire to burn for 10 minutes before making any damper adjustments. I do not add any smoking wood. Both the bottom vent and daisy wheel should now be open about 80 percent. The target smoking temperature is about 600°F (315°C) as indicated on your dome thermometer. It is okay if you overshoot the target temperature. Just know that the hotter the fire, the less time will be needed to cook.

Pizza setup is very important. Place the plate setter legs up, add the grill grate and then add the pizza stone. An air gap between the plate setter and the stone is very important for air circulation as well as for shielding the stone from getting too hot. Allow the grill to preheat for a minimum of 35 to 40 minutes to ensure the ceramic is hot.

Flour a dough scraper and use it to scoop up one of the dough balls and drop the dough into a bowl of flour. Flip the dough to cover both sides completely. Shake off any excess flour and place the dough on a clean work surface. Use your fingers to press down the center of the dough ball. Press outward to deflate all the air from the dough. Once it is large enough, use the palms of your hands to stretch the dough all the way around to form a 14-inch (35-cm)-diameter pie. Sprinkle a pinch of semolina flour onto a wooden pizza peel. Carefully transfer the dough to the peel. Top with about ⅓ cup (81 g) of Grandma Marie's pizza sauce, then add pinches of fresh mozzarella cheese and basil and give it a thin swirl of extra virgin olive oil.

Place the wooden peel on the pizza stone, slowly start to move the peel back and forth, then slide the pizza directly onto the stone. Cook for 5 minutes, or until the edges are golden and the cheese is melted. Repeat to prepare the other 3 pizzas.

CHICAGO-STYLE DEEP-DISH PIZZA

Deep-dish pizza is a must when we visit family in Chicago. My favorite has to be Gino's East. Their slab o' sausage pizza is absolutely amazing. Before Gino's opened its Atlanta location, I was forced to create my own.

MAKES ONE 12" (35-CM) PIZZA; SERVES 5 OR 6

DEEP-DISH PIZZA CRUST

2¼ tsp (9 g) active dry yeast

1 tbsp (15 ml) honey

1¼ cups (295 ml) room-temperature water

3¼ cups (406 g) all-purpose flour, plus more for dusting

½ cup (70 g) cornmeal

1 tbsp (18 g) salt

3 tbsp (42 g) unsalted butter, melted

Olive oil

½ cup (112 g/1 stick) unsalted butter

PREPARE THE CRUST:

In a small bowl, combine the yeast and honey with the water. Stir and allow the yeast to rehydrate for 15 minutes. It should froth up quite a bit.

In a large bowl, combine the flour, cornmeal and salt. Whisk together thoroughly. Add the melted butter and yeast mixture and stir thoroughly. Once all the ingredients have come together and the dough is hard to stir, turn out the mixture onto a floured surface. Knead for 5 to 6 minutes, or until the dough has come together in a smooth ball. Place in a lightly oiled bowl and allow it to proof for 1 hour. Cover with a clean towel and place in a draft-free, warm spot. While the dough proofs, set out the ½ cup (112 g/1 stick) of butter to soften it.

When the proofing time is over, turn out the dough ball onto a floured surface. Using a rolling pin, roll out as thinly as possible. (The shape does not matter.) Spread the softened butter evenly all over the entire top surface of the thinned dough.

Carefully, roll out the dough, fold each end over and reshape into a ball. This is creating buttered layers to make a perfect, buttery crust. Return the dough ball to the oiled bowl. Roll the dough ball inside the bowl to coat with oil. (This will stop the dough from forming a skin.) Cover with a clean towel and return it to the draft-free, warm spot for at least 1 more hour before cooking.

(CONTINUED)

CHICAGO-STYLE DEEP-DISH PIZZA (CONTINUED)

TO ASSEMBLE

2 tbsp (30 ml) extra virgin olive oil

8 slices mozzarella

8 oz (225 g) shredded mozzarella cheese

Grandma Marie's Pizza Sauce (page 133)

Shaved Parmesan cheese

Fresh basil (optional)

SUGGESTED TOPPINGS

Pepperoni, chopped (I prefer Boar's Head brand)

Italian sausage

Mushrooms

Dried basil

BIG GREEN EGG SETUP:

Fill your firebox with natural lump charcoal and prepare your Big Green Egg for indirect cooking. Both the daisy wheel and bottom vent should be wide open during ignition. Use a torch or starter cubes to light the charcoal in a single spot to start a bed of coals. Allow the fire to burn for 10 minutes before making any damper adjustments. I don't use smoking wood when baking. Wet batters tend to absorb a ton of smoke, which does not taste great in breads and desserts. Both the bottom vent and daisy wheel should now be open about 30 percent. The target smoking temperature is about 425°F (220°C) as indicated on your dome thermometer. It is okay if you overshoot the target temperature. Just know that the hotter the fire, the less time will be needed to cook.

Turn out the dough ball onto a lightly floured surface after the dough has completed proofing. Using a rolling pin, evenly roll out the dough as close to a 12-inch (30-cm)-diameter circle as possible. Pour 2 tablespoons (30 ml) of extra virgin olive oil into a 12-inch (30-cm) cast-iron skillet and swirl to coat the entire bottom. Carefully transfer your crust into the skillet. Shape and form the crust to fit perfectly in the cast-iron skillet. Cut off any excess dough that protrudes past the edge of the skillet.

Building a deep-dish pizza is backward from a traditional pizza. Place the sliced mozzarella in first, then sprinkle in your shredded mozzarella cheese, making sure it covers evenly. Then, add your preferred toppings.

Now, add the sauce. Use the back of a spoon to help spread it evenly. Top with a bit of shaved Parmesan cheese. (I also added fresh basil.)

Bake inside the Big Green Egg for 20 to 25 minutes, or until the crust is golden brown and firm to the touch. Remember that the cast-iron skillet will be extremely hot!

Remove from the grill and allow the pizza to cool and set up for a minimum of 20 minutes before slicing and serving.

JALAPEÑO CHEDDAR CORNBREAD

Cornbread comes in various shapes, sizes and crumbs. I prefer a moist cornbread and anything with some heat is better, in my opinion. Here's my recipe.

SERVES 6 TO 8

5 tbsp (70 g) unsalted butter

1 cup (115 g) shredded sharp Cheddar cheese, divided

DRY INGREDIENTS

1¼ cups (175 g) cornmeal

¾ cup (90 g) all-purpose flour

¼ cup (50 g) sugar

½ tsp kosher salt

½ tsp baking soda

2 tsp (9 g) baking powder

WET INGREDIENTS

2 large eggs

1 cup (240 ml) buttermilk

¼ cup (60 g) sour cream

¼ cup (30 g) diced pickled jalapeño peppers

¼ cup (60 ml) milk

BIG GREEN EGG SETUP:

Fill your firebox with natural lump charcoal and prepare your Big Green Egg for indirect cooking. Both the daisy wheel and bottom vent should be wide open during ignition. Use a torch or starter cubes to light the charcoal in a single spot to start a bed of coals. Allow the fire to burn for 10 minutes before making any damper adjustments. I don't use smoking wood when baking. Wet batters tend to absorb a ton of smoke, which does not taste great in breads and desserts. Both the bottom vent and daisy wheel should now be open about 40 percent. The target smoking temperature is about 425°F (220°C) as indicated on your dome thermometer. It is okay if you overshoot the target temperature. Just know that the hotter the fire, the less time will be needed to cook.

Heat a 10-inch (25-cm) cast-iron skillet over low heat on the stovetop. Drop in the butter to melt. Swirl the butter all over the skillet. Make sure you get the sides of the skillet so that your cornbread doesn't stick.

In a medium bowl, thoroughly whisk together all the dry ingredients. Pour the melted butter from the skillet into the dry ingredients. Add the wet ingredients and ¾ cup (85 g) of the Cheddar cheese and mix well.

Pour the mixture into the warm skillet. Give the skillet a shake to ensure an even thickness and to prevent any air pockets. Top evenly with the remaining ¼ cup (30 g) of cheese.

Bake on the grill for 23 to 27 minutes, or until golden brown. Remove from the grill and allow to cool for 10 minutes before slicing.

TORTA DE RON
(CHOCOLATE RUM CAKE)

Chocolate cake is one of my family's favorites. This recipe is tender, moist and one of the tastiest chocolate cakes I've eaten.

SERVES 10 TO 12

2 tbsp (28 g) unsalted butter, for pan

¼ cup (30 g) all-purpose flour, for pan

4 large eggs

1 cup (230 g) sour cream

1 (18.25-oz [517-g]) box yellow cake mix

1 tsp pure vanilla extract

½ cup (120 ml) canola oil

1 (5.9-oz [167-g]) box instant chocolate pudding mix

¼ cup (60 ml) rum

1 cup (175 g) semisweet chocolate chips

Confectioners' sugar, for dusting

BIG GREEN EGG SETUP:

Fill your firebox with natural lump charcoal and prepare your Big Green Egg for indirect cooking. Both the daisy wheel and bottom vent should be wide open during ignition. Use a torch or starter cubes to light the charcoal in a single spot to start a bed of coals. Allow the fire to burn for 10 minutes before making any damper adjustments. I don't use smoking wood when baking. Wet batters tend to absorb a ton of smoke, which does not taste great in breads and desserts. Both the bottom vent and daisy wheel should now be open about 30 percent. The target smoking temperature is about 350°F (180°C) as indicated on your dome thermometer. It is okay if you overshoot the target temperature. Just know that the hotter the fire, the less time will be needed to cook.

Use the butter to butter a Bundt pan. Use your hand to get it into every single nook and cranny of the pan. Add the flour and shake the pan, coating all of the butter with the flour. Once all the butter has been covered, tap the outside of the pan with your hand to loosen any excess flour and discard. These steps will aid in a smooth release of the cake from the pan when cooked through.

In a large bowl, combine the eggs, sour cream, cake mix, vanilla, oil, pudding mix and rum and beat for 10 minutes, using a mixer on low speed. Then, add the chocolate chips and mix until evenly incorporated. Pour the cake batter into the prepared Bundt pan. Use a spatula to smooth and even out the batter. Place the pan in the center of the grill and bake for 40 to 45 minutes, rotating the Bundt pan 180 degrees halfway through the cook. Use a wooden skewer or toothpick to probe down inside the cake. If it comes out clean, the cake is done. Remove from the grill and allow the cake to cool in its pan for 3 minutes. Place the plate of a cake stand upside down against the open rim of the pan. Hold both the plate and pan and flip the cake with one smooth, quick flip. The cake should fall out of the pan and land on the plate. Allow the cake to cool for a minimum of 30 minutes. Dump some confectioners' sugar into a sieve and dust over the cake just before serving.

MAPLE BACON OATMEAL COOKIES

It's no secret, I love bacon. I love it for breakfast, I love it on a burger, I love it in desserts! These cookies have been crowd-pleasers at BBQ events.

SERVES 10 TO 12

8 oz (225 g) bacon

½ cup (112 g/1 stick) unsalted butter, at room temperature

½ cup (100 g) granulated sugar

½ cup (115 g) light brown sugar

1 large egg

½ tsp pure vanilla extract

1 cup (125 g) all-purpose flour

½ tsp baking soda

½ tsp salt

1 tsp ground cinnamon

1½ cups (120 g) quick-cooking oats

GLAZE

1¾ cups (210 g) confectioners' sugar

3 tbsp (45 ml) water

3 tbsp (45 ml) pure maple syrup

In a large skillet over medium-high heat, fry the bacon. Allow to cool, chop and set aside. In a large bowl, combine the butter and the granulated and brown sugar and beat with an electric mixer on medium speed until fluffy. Beat in the egg and vanilla until combined.

In a separate bowl, whisk together the flour, baking soda, salt and cinnamon. Slowly stir the flour mixture into the butter mixture. Gradually stir in the oats and bacon. Cover and refrigerate for at least 1 hour.

BIG GREEN EGG SETUP:

Fill your firebox with natural lump charcoal and prepare your Big Green Egg for indirect cooking. Both the daisy wheel and bottom vent should be wide open during ignition. Use a torch or starter cubes to light the charcoal in a single spot to start a bed of coals. Allow the fire to burn for 10 minutes before making any damper adjustments. I don't use smoking wood when baking. Wet batters tend to absorb a ton of smoke, which does not taste great in breads and desserts. Both the bottom vent and daisy wheel should now be open about 30 percent. The target smoking temperature is about 375°F (190°C) as indicated on your dome thermometer. It is okay if you overshoot the target temperature. Just know that the hotter the fire, the less time will be needed to cook.

Scoop about ¼ cup (60 g) of the dough and roll into a ball. Use a fork dipped in water to slightly flatten the balls. Place on an ungreased cookie sheet.

Cook for 10 to 12 minutes, or until golden brown. Remove from the grill and allow the cookies to cool on their cookie sheet for several minutes before transferring to a cooling rack.

PREPARE THE GLAZE:

In a small bowl, mix together all the glaze ingredients until smooth and allow to sit for about 5 minutes. Drizzle the glaze over the cookies while they are on the cooling rack.

ACKNOWLEDGMENTS

To my beautiful wife, Elise. Thank you for putting up with all of the craziness that I choose to endure. Thank you for waiting on me to capture the perfect shot and having to eat cold dinners. Thank you for giving me the opportunity to pursue my vision. You are my rock.

I want to thank my mother, Ann Tabor, for her amazing support during the cookbook photo shoot. She washed every single dish, sometimes several times. This would have been impossible without her. Thank you, Mom.

I'd like to thank Scott and Alicia Wehner for all of their help setting up the stage. Their help was essential in getting the stage set for the shoot. Thank you for all that you do.

To all of my friends and neighbors who stopped in to eat, held screens and aided with whatever I needed, thank you all.

Thanks to all the Page Street Publishing crew for making this so enjoyable. Their professionalism and experience are what make them successful.

Ken Goodman's eye and lens are a fantastically amazing combination of talent. Thank you for making my food look remarkable.

ABOUT THE AUTHOR

Craig is a chef playing the role of a backyard BBQ warrior. His slogan, "There isn't anything I won't grill," is a dead-on representation of how he approaches outdoor cooking. Craig has mastered the BBQ staples, such as pork shoulder, brisket and ribs, but his skill and commitment to all foods coal-fired extends to chef-inspired dishes, such as beef Wellington, paella and sushi. Yes, he has made grilled sushi before!

Craig is an equal opportunity griller. He owns five Big Green Eggs, a Kamado Joe, a FLO Kamado, a REC TEC Pellet smoker and the classic backyard staple, a Weber Kettle. That said, his true passion is cooking on the Big Green Egg, the reason for his internationally known moniker. Craig has won the national Big Green Egg festival's top honor (Eggtoberfest's People's Choice Award) in back-to-back years.

Craig can be found on the web at www.craigtabor.com, on numerous BBQ forums under the handle @craigtabor or on Instagram under the same name, where his followers drool with each daily upload from the grill master himself.

INDEX

Tequila Lime Steak Tacos with Fire-Roasted Corn Salsa, 80–83

Torta De Ron (Chocolate Rum Cake), 140

Trimming

brisket, 25–27

chicken halves, 30

fat from pork shoulder, 36, 39

of spare ribs, 41, 42

Tri Tip Sandwich, Pastrami'd, 74–76

Turkey Breast, Texas-Style Smoked, 33–35

Turkey Leg, Disney-Style, 64

Twice-Smoked Taters, 122

V

Valencia rice, in Seafood Paella, 105–107

Vidalia onion

Pastrami'd Tri Tip Sandwich, 74–76

Smo-Fried Wings with Habanero BBQ Sauce, 49–50

Smoked Apple Baked Beans, 121

W

Water pans, 28

Whiskey, in Jack Daniel's Tennessee Honey–Glazed Cedar-Planked Salmon, 95–96

White fish, in Cioppino, 101–102

White vinegar

Hot Smoked Tater Salad, 129

Patrami'd Tri Tip Sandwich, 74–76

White wine, in Cioppino, 101–102

Wired thermometer, 14, 28, 29, 32, 35, 36

Worcestershire sauce

Cowboy Burger, 77–79

Smo-Fried Wings with Habanero BBQ Sauce, 49–50

Smoked Apple Baked Beans, 121

Steak Kebabs with Chinese Garlic Sauce, 63

Wrapping/wrapped

beef brisket, 27, 29

Boston Butt (Pork Shoulder), 39

pork ribs, 45

Tomahawk rib eye, 52

Y

Yeast

Chicago-Style Deep-Dish Pizza, 135–136

Neapolitan-Style Pizza, 133–134

Yellow cake mix, in Torta De Ron (Chocolate Rum Cake), 140

Yellow mustard

Asian BBQ Shrimp, 67

Cowboy Burger, 77–79

Smoked Apple Baked Beans, 121